CASTROCHAVISM

Organized Crime in the Americas

CARLOS SANCHEZ BERZAIN

Interamerican Institute for Democracy Editorial Found

Translated from Spanish by:
Edgar L. Terrazas, Traducciones LLC, ATA # 234680.

Diesign: www.alexlib.com

Interamerican Institute for Democracy Editorial Found
2100 Coral Way. Ste. 500
Miami, FL 33145
U.S.A.
Tel: (786) 409-4554
Fax: (786) 409-4576
www.intdemocratic.org
iid@intdemocratic.org

To the persecuted, prisoners and political exiles, to the families of those killed and to all the victims of transnational organized crime that is "castrochavism", with the promise that there will be justice and and impunity will end.

CONTENTS

7. ARMED FORCES

1

CONCEPTS and HISTORY

CASTROCHAVISMO
Organized Crime in the Américas[1]

Carlos Sánchez Berzain

The author has a long list of publications devoted to the emergence of the new criminal States in Latin America. Below we publish the presentation speech he made to his latest book: "Castrochavismo". Sánchez believes this is the name that best describes the transnational organized crime system that usurps political power in Cuba, Venezuela, Bolivia and Nicaragua, which should be treated as an organized crime structure and not as a political process. The gravity, recurrence, and impunity of the crimes committed by Castro-Díaz-Canel, Maduro, Morales, Ortega-Murillo and the members of their regimes, added to the transnational structure they have developed, has reduced the oppressed peoples to a "defenseless condition" and represents the most serious threat to peace and security in the Americas.

The dictatorships that exist today in Cuba, Venezuela, Bolivia and Nicaragua, based on the partnership between Hugo Chavez and Fidel Castro, are a structure of "transnational organized crime" and not a political process. This points to a fundamental legal, social, and security issue. It is about the continuation of a battle for the truth, starting by calling things by their name, in order to recognize and understand reality objectively and with realism.

---

1. Book of the same title by Carlos Sánchez Berzain, August 2019

In the 21st century, the international community, the governments, the academia, the free press and society, have been reluctant -and some still are- to recognize that dictatorships have multiplied in the Americas and that instead of one dictatorship, that of Cuba, that existed alone in 1999, twenty years later there are four dictatorships that have democracies under permanent threat and conspiracy.

One of my first books in this field is *XXI Century Dictatorship in Bolivia,* [2] which demonstrates with documents that a dictatorship was installed in Bolivia as of 2006. This book retakes and develops the concept of dictatorships that reach power through elections and through successive coups liquidate democracy, first broached by Oswaldo Hurtado, the former President of Ecuador, who wrote *Las Dictaduras del siglo XXI: caso Ecuador* (2012).

In my book *Dictatorship and Democracy in the Americas,*[3] I set out to reflect on and demonstrate the existence of two Americas. Not two Americas from a cultural point of view -Latin versus Anglo-Saxon-, not two Americas either from the economic point of view -first world versus third world-, nor two Americas differentiated by their degree of development -developed versus underdeveloped or developing-, two Americas, not even socially speaking, but two Americas organized and divided by their essential elements and conditions of democracy. A group of dictatorships led by Cuba and made up by Venezuela, Nicaragua, Bolivia, and Rafael Correa's Ecuador, and aligned to the Kirchners' Argentina, to the Brazil of the Workers Party and Lula/Rousseff, and with a very widespread presence and control in Central America with PetroCaribe, and the Organization of American States (OAS).

The two Americas make up an axis of confrontation in which perpetual and arbitrary control of power on the one hand, branded

2. Sanchez Berzain, Carlos. *XXI Century Dictatorship in Bolivia.* Editorial Fund, Interamerican Institute for Democracy. Amazon.com. 2013
3. Sánchez Berzain, Carlos. *Dictatorship and Democracy in the Americas.* Editorial Fund, Interamerican Institute for Democracy. Amazon.com. 2017

dictatorships with ideology as a pretext; versus democracy, with respect for human rights, alternation in power, accountability and free elections, declaratively protected by the inter-American system, enshrined -among others- in the inter-American democratic charter.

Now I introduce "Castrochavismo", a neologism, a single word. A word that represents two characters that have marked the history of early 21st century in the Americas: Castro and Chávez. I accompany the title with a phrase that, in addition to pointing out the fundamental characteristic of those named, is a definition. "Organized Crime in the Americas" describes the system of institutionalized, recurring, trans-national and unpunished crime, as a form of power management and usurpation in States under dictatorial control. Today, they are Cuba with Raúl Castro-Díaz-Canel, Venezuela with Nicolás Maduro, Bolivia with Evo Morales and Nicaragua with Daniel Ortega-Rosario Murillo.

This is a story that you all know well but I will retell it anyway. In 1999 there was only one dictatorship in the Americas: Castro's in Cuba. After 40 years of holding power, he was going through the worst of what he called a Special Period. His project was dying: the new decade had seen the Berlin Wall fall, and the Soviet Union was destroyed; and as a consequence his own dictatorship had been left without auspices and economic support, as the parasitic entity that it always was. Then it happened that Colonel Hugo Chávez won the presidential elections and took charge of the Venezuelan government. A coup monger, flattered and protected by Fidel Castro, he immediately ran to Cuba and formed or reactivated an alliance, a criminal society, which at the beginning was imperceptible, but that has changed and branded the history of the 21st century in the Americas. Thus was created what today we should call Castrochavismo.

From 1959 to 1999, the Cuban dictatorship is "Castroism." From 1999 onwards, it is "Castrochavismo," led by Hugo Chavez until his death. As of the alliance with Chávez, the new project recognized his clear leadership due to the contribution and control of Venezuela's money and oil, used as the main instruments for maneuvering, coercion, destabilization and bribery. It began as progressive leftist populism, and was successively called ALBA Movement (Bolivarian Alliance for the Peoples of Our America, in Spanish); Bolivarian Movement; after a few years Socialism of the 21st Century, and nowadays Castrochavismo. Since its inception, Castrochavismo sought to pose as a political, populist and democratic movement, but on the basis of facts and the objective reality, such characteristics were only a disguise, an alibi or a mask to hide the true nature of the greatest group of transnational organized crime to hold political power.

When in 1999 Chávez and Castro united, a very fragile Chávez, with an unstable government, sought stability and political support. These he got with Castro's dictatorial security system and his repression services, which would end up being imposed on Venezuela. Fidel Castro receives money and oil to get Cuba out of famine, and resumes his failed and dying project, that he calls "Revolution". With this he had controlled Cuba since 1959, had covered with blood the Americas with the guerrillas of the 60s, he had continued to shedw blood in the 70s and 80s with the urban guerrillas, sabotage, narco guerrillas and terrorism. He even went beyond the Americas to Angola, but that was inoperable because the source of Soviet financing collapsed, thus putting an end to the Cold War.

Castro receives a new source of financing for his conspiratorial and criminal actions with Chávez's surrender not only of Venezuela's money and oil but, as we have learned today, of the entire country. This allows the only dictator at the time to reactivate genuine Castroism under the mantle of the Bolivarian movement or ALBA project, and disguise it as democracy; with Venezuela's money, he started conspiracies, which led to the fall and overthrow of democratic leaders. The first one occurs in Argentina, with the fall of President

De La Rúa; the second happens in Ecuador and it is Jamil Mahuad who pays the price; the third one is the overthrow of President Gonzalo Sánchez de Lozada in Bolivia; the fourth is in Ecuador, with the fall of President Lucio Gutiérrez. They also overthrew the OAS Secretary General, Miguel Ángel Rodríguez, who had just been elected. A false case of corruption was planted in Costa Rica, where Rodríguez ends up being illegally detained, making room for Insulsa to arrive. The rest is known history, the dominance and leadership of Latin America by Chavez until his death and then by Cuba's Castro dictators.

With the new century, Chávez and Castro started on a path of destroying democracy in the Americas, promptly aggravated by the terrorist attacks of September 11, 2001 against the United States. As a result, the region got politically abandoned by the country leader of democracy. The nascent Castrochavista organization expands with Lula da Silva taking power in Brazil with the Workers' Party, whose government he used to strengthen the extraordinary flow of economic resources with transnational corruption. A sample of such crimes is the infamous case "Lava Jato-Odebrecht," among others.

The destruction of democracy becomes noticeable: the exiles, who had been purely Cuban, became regional with Venezuelans, Bolivians, Nicaraguans, Ecuadorians, Argentineans, and Central Americans. The former President Oswaldo Hurtado from Ecuador points out the issue in view of Rafael Correa's overrun against institutions and the Republic. I denounced the existence and consolidation of the dictatorship of Morales in Bolivia. Carlos Alberto Montaner, from his columns and programs, notes the expansion of the Castro power. Armando Valladares, in his lectures and denunciations calls them out, and many other authors testify to the proliferation of dictatorial regimes promoted by Chávez and Castro. These works, lectures and forums attract attention, but there is a reaction of disbelief with the argument that the dictatorships articulated by Chavez and Castro continued to be democracies because they held elections. Elections in Venezuela, elections in Nicaragua, elections in Ecuador and Bolivia, but bypassing and hiding that they had destroyed all the legal and constitutional order, finished the rule of law and created a reality with infamous laws [4] - that violate human rights and eliminate the fundamental guarantees - to establish a quasi-legal regime that is criminal.

It is important to remember that the Inter-American Democratic Charter, signed in Lima on September 11th, 2001 by all the countries in the Americas, with the exception of the Cuban dictatorship, has mandatory value for the member States of the OAS. It is a mandatory instrument deliberately ignored throughout the period of control of the OAS by Castrochavismo under Secretary General Insulza and partially applied in the recent tenure.

The Inter-American Democratic Charter establishes in its First Article that "The peoples of the Americas have the right to democracy and their governments have the obligation to promote and defend it." Article Third mandates that "Essential elements of representative democracy include, *inter alia*, respect for human rights and fundamental freedoms, access to and exercise of power in accordance with the rule of law, the holding of periodic, free, and fair elections based on secret balloting and universal suffrage as an expression of the sovereignty of the people, the pluralistic system of political parties and organizations, and the separation of powers and independence of the branches of government.

---

4. "Infamous Law is a norm that, elaborated and established following the formal procedure for its creation, violates in its object or contents the human rights or fundamental freedoms." They are laws that the Castrochavista regimes approve with the control they have of the Legislative Power, uphold with their command of constitutionality control, and apply with the control they have of the prosecutors and judges of the regime. In "Political Prisoners of Organized Crime Regimes," Carlos Sánchez Berzain. Infobae May 28, 2018

Since 2003, in my writings, conferences, press statements, academic papers and books, I repeatedly maintain that the absence of only one of the "essential" elements makes democracy disappear, and that in countries with governments established by Castro and Chávez, as in Venezuela, Ecuador under Correa, Bolivia with Morales, and Nicaragua with Ortega, none of the essential elements of democracy are met or exist, with the aggravating element that they all have political prisoners and exiles, legalized persecution and have liquidated freedom of the press.

Today's elections are used as a means of simulation even in Cuba, which has just falsified the reform of a constitution that is a mere statute of control by the dictatorship. The manipulation of electoral processes with the existence of none of the essential elements of democracy by Castrochavismo is another chain of crimes that leads us to a concept that I propose to be studied by political science, that of "electoral dictatorship".

An electoral dictatorship is a "political regime that by force or violence concentrates all power in a person or in a group or organization that represses human rights and fundamental freedoms and uses illegitimate elections, neither free nor fair, with fraud and corruption, to perpetuate itself indefinitely in power". It is an expression of a chain of crimes that usurp the popular will and the sovereignty of the peoples. In an electoral dictatorship "you vote, but you don't elect." Watch out, "you vote, but you don't elect", in order to simulate democracy and claim international legitimacy, with well lubricated propaganda and manipulation mechanisms by some international organizations. It has worked for them although with increasing difficulties because crimes are already in evidence, and citizens in resistance and rebellion.

In the history of Castrochavismo, it went through an initial stage in which it was called Socialism of the 21st Century, covered with ideology to pose as a progressive and democratic project. It tried unsuccessfully to survive operating within the Sao Paulo Forum, an instrument that appears as a leftist group organized by Cuba in response to the collapse of the Soviet Union. It also creates bodies and organizations claiming to be populist, or leftist, claiming to be progressive, socialist, and some even communist, always trying to stay in the field of politics, when actually it was about covering up a criminal structure.

In these 20 years of Castrochavismo, a very interesting phenomenon occurs in the transformation of pure Castroism to Castrochavismo. The leader, the boss, was the one who put the money and that was unquestionably Hugo Chávez, but it turns out that Chávez dies -very conveniently for the Cuban dictatorship- and the Castros and Cuba assume the leadership, and that command leads them to the leadership of Latin America, first to the OAS Summit in Panama where there is an encounter with the president of the United States, and an opening that recognizes such leadership of the oldest dictatorship in Latin America. If Chavez had still been alive, surely the term would be Chávezcastrismo, but today the criminal group is under the clear and indisputable leadership of Raúl Castro and Cuba.

Cuba, separated from the OAS for violating freedom, democracy and being a threat against international peace and security, is almost begged to be reinstated to the OAS, and without accepting reinstatement goes to the Panama summit in command of the Latin American countries against the US, with the express recognition of the latter. And after the Panama summit, that enshrines the leadership of Latin America in the hands of Castro and Cuba, what ensues is the opening of relations between the US and the visit of the US president to Cuba. Without a doubt, the moment of greatest political triumph of organized crime over democracy.

During this 21st century, Latin America has had two clear leaderships. First Hugo Chávez, who acted as the undisputed leader because he was handling money and privilege, having Fidel Castro as a kind of oracle in Havana, where all the heads of State and government paid homage visits. The death of Chavez, who at some point must be the subject of a serious historical investigation for the extraordinary benefit and power that it leaves to Cuba, determines the change of power at the hands of the Castros, from Venezuela to Cuba, until they entered into crisis.

I maintain that today Latin America does not have a leadership and that a fight is being waged that is no longer the confrontation that I narrated in my book on the two Americas, between dictatorship and democracy. There are still two Americas that confront each other, but now they are one democratic America, and another controlled by a criminal organization. The confrontation is expressed with a permanent conspiracy, threats against the security and integrity of the States, terrorism, drug trafficking, human rights violations, crimes against humanity, crimes against nature, devastation of natural and protected resources and more.

That criminal Castrochavista America, which is not political, is the objective of this book in which, through case studies, analysis, columns, essays and data of the objective reality, I show that the Castrochavismo that today controls Cuba, Venezuela, Bolivia and Nicaragua under the figure of dictatorships, electoral dictatorships or dictatorships of transnational organized crime, is a criminal entity that must be separated from politics and must be treated as transnational organized crime within the framework of the Palermo Convention [5] and other norms, without the immunities or privileges inherent to the heads of State or government.

Castrochavismo had the leadership of Latin America with Chávez, and then with the Castros, but they enter into a crisis because the

---

5. United Nations, year 2000. United Nations Convention against Transnational Organized Crime (Palermo Convention), a multilateral treaty.

peoples begin to have problems; because the statist and criminal model of these regimes leads to a crisis, and they are very bad administrators with hyper corruption. They have dissipated the wealth of Venezuela; the high prices of raw materials that helped them no longer exist; peoples fight for their freedom and internal conflicts appear, and thus they lose control of much of the region. They also lose control of the OAS.

The dictatorships of Castrochavismo are today in a critical situation, making great efforts to survive, following the model of the Cuban dictatorship that boasts about 60 years in power. This is a new scenario, a defense scenario in which Castrochavismo, instead of maintaining its expansion, has been exhausted, is in evidence, and has been reduced to the control of Cuba, Venezuela, Bolivia and Nicaragua. The last loss is that of Ecuador, that thanks to the vision of the candidate and successor to dictator Correa, the current president Lenin Moreno, has clearly left that group.

Castrochavista dictatorships are in crisis but not defeated. They are called out as regimes that violate human rights, that have no rule of law, where there is no division or independence of public powers, and that are narco States and creators of poverty. To remain in power, they apply the uniform strategy of "resisting at all costs, destabilizing democracies, politicizing their situation and negotiating." The strategic leadership is that of the Cuban dictatorship, that has converted the exercise of organized crime from the power of a State into a social and political control methodology and has expanded these practices to Venezuela, Nicaragua and Bolivia, operated by Cuban personnel.

The first element of its strategy, of "retention of power at all costs," can be seen in Nicaragua and how many people they have tortured, imprisoned and killed last year; in Venezuela, where the same happens; in Cuba, where they repress and with political prisoners and crimes all the time. Let's see Bolivia, from where the president of the human rights assembly has just reported that there are 131 deaths without investigating, for killings that the government has committed, and more than 100 political prisoners; and that UNHCR, the United Nations High Commissioner for Refugees, has registered more than 1,200 Bolivians exiled in Brazil, Peru, United States, Spain and Paraguay.

The second element of their strategy is to "destabilize democracies," for which they conspire against those who accuse them and against the governments that defend democracy. There is conspiracy from Argentina to the US; there is a conspiracy in Peru, there is a conspiracy in Panama, there is conspiracy in Colombia, where now the FARC resume their armed struggle; there is a conspiracy in Brazil, because they have a lot of money to exacerbate genuine claims that there may be in society and turn them into actions of political destabilization with which they negotiate and extort. The destabilization ranges from false news and character assassination of leaders whom they designate as right-wing, to criminal acts of terrorism, kidnappings and narco guerrillas.

The third element of their strategy is to "politicize their situation and their criminal acts" and that has to do with this book. When the dictatorships in Cuba, Venezuela, Bolivia, Nicaragua, improperly imprison a citizen, when they torture them, when they even kill them, they call it defense of the revolution. It is not murder, it is not torture, it is not crime, it is to defend the revolution, and thus they build their causes of criminal justification. The four dictatorships are narco States and, to justify themselves, they argue that "drug trafficking is an instrument of struggle for the liberation of the peoples", repeating and refining the fallacy that began with Fidel Castro in the 60s, repeated by Che Guevara, and proclaimed by Evo Morales in 2016 at the United Nations, saying that "the fight against drug trafficking is an instrument of imperialism to oppress the peoples". That is to say, in revolutionary terms, criminally in Castrochavismo, there is justification for all crimes. If there is any doubt, let's see what just happened to the criminal drug dealer who has fled from Colombia to Venezuela: Jesús Santrich has proclaimed himself as being persecuted by the right, and by the *tremendously fierce* government of Colombia, when this is a criminal who should be in jail, because even after signing the peace treaty he was trafficking, and he was filmed and photographed, and there can be no more truthful evidence than that. Or how about the bosses of the ELN narco guerrilla of Colombia, under protection in Cuba! This third element in the strategy of Castrochavismo, which consists in politicizing their crimes, serves to ensure that when they kill any person they say that they are defending the revolution, when they torture they say they defend the popular process of liberation of peoples and so on. They commit more crimes every day to keep the previous ones in impunity and continue to hold power.

And the fourth element of the Castrochavista strategy is to "negotiate." They negotiate in order to gain time, demoralize the adversary, collect bills from their allies or extort money from third States to gain their support or at least neutralize them. They make a good mix of these four elements and are surviving that way.

Among the many cases that prove that the dictatorships of Cuba, Venezuela, Bolivia and Nicaragua are organized crime and nothing political, those of Cuba stand out. They present as a notable example the "trafficking of slave doctors by Cuba", with the alibi of internationalism for the cooperation and liberation of the peoples, when in fact far from being social aid for Brazilians, Bolivians, Ecuadorians, Venezuelans, where they send doctors, it is genuine 21st century slavery. For each doctor or professional, the Cuban dictatorship appropriates more than 80% of the salaries paid for them, and the poor doctors are slaves that have their families as hostages in Cuba; they have to surrender passports, and everything mediated by the Pan

American Health Organization, at the service of a crime typified and condemned by the second annex to the Palermo Convention.

In Brazil, thanks to the decision by President Bolsonaro, the trafficking of people, with slave doctors in the "Mais Médicos" program has ceased, but there are still doctors and other types of Cuban slaves in Bolivia, Venezuela, Nicaragua and another six dozen countries. That is organized crime, but it continues to receive such legitimacy as if we were dealing with a political event, a relationship between governments to traffic people, even an act of cooperation, instead of clearly calling it out as a criminal act.

Other crimes of Castrochavismo that are "public and notorious facts" are drug trafficking, simulation and electoral fraud, torture and murder, and political prisoners and exiles, attacks on freedom of the press, corruption and illicit enrichment, with family members and their entourage exhibiting their ill-gained fortunes around the world, criminal associations to launder resources from criminal activities, confiscations of private property (we must remember that private property is a human right proclaimed by Article 19 of the Universal Declaration of Human Rights). All that and more is pure crime, and it is not political.

I insist that political events are based on respect for the "rule of law," which is simply that "no one is above the law," on the temporality of public service, on accountability and public responsibility, where you can take on an adversary. But organized crime has no adversaries, it has enemies and the difference between an adversary and an enemy is that the former is defeated or convinced, whereas the latter is eliminated, and this explains the number of crimes that Castrochavismo commits in the Americas.

The criminal handling by these dictatorships of crimes against the freedom of people is happening in Nicaragua, where the regime takes prisoners, negotiates their freedom, and releases prisoners to take them back, and manages that dynamic to intimidate people. The same has been the case in Venezuela, where there are hundreds of political prisoners. Castrochavista dictatorships have manipulated justice as a mechanism for persecution and political repression, another area of their criminal activity. With this, in addition to demonstrating that there is no division or independence of powers, they violate virtually all people's rights. The "legalization of political repression" is another concept resulting from the criminal nature of Castrochavismo.

One of the examples closest to me of what organized crime action means is currently being carried out in my country, Bolivia, where Castrochavismo repeats an *iter criminis* already perpetrated in Venezuela and Nicaragua. *Iter criminis* means "the process of development of a crime", it is the "path that an offender goes through from the moment he intends to perpetrate a crime, through the preparation and carrying out of the intermediate steps of the crime until the criminal act is completed."

In Bolivia there are elections on October 20th. Castrochavista elections are electoral dictatorship, where you vote but you do not elect. A brief summary of the crimes that have been committed and continue to be committed: Evo Morales supplanted the political constitution of the State and liquidated the Republic of Bolivia in 2009, by establishing a constitution that gives birth to a plurinational State. In that constitution that is founded on falsifications, massacres and exile, because thus he had his constitution approved, he states that he can only be reelected once, only once; then in 2009 he is immediately elected, and when that mandate expired in 2014, he goes back to re-election. He can no longer be reelected, but Morales asks for an interpretation by his Constitutional Court, and it says that the Republic of Bolivia having been extinguished, and the plurinational State been born in 2009, Evo Morales has only been elected once in the plurinational State; that is, this is his first reelection and he can run again in 2014. That is to say they criminally simulate that Morales never came to the presidency in the Republic of Bolivia, committing a crime of prevarication and a crime of falsehood of material, ideological falsehood, and genuine organized crime.

We are not talking about politics, because if it were political there would be a constitutional body, a supreme court, to exercise constitutional control and to say that it cannot happen because that is not under the "rule of law." But in organized crime, the judgments are characterized by prevarication, and the judges are only instruments dependent on power and at its service. But the criminal chain continues, and Evo Morales after being illegally re-elected in 2014, makes a referendum seeking indefinite reelection, and despite fraud and manipulation on February 21st, 2016, he loses. Bolivia said NO. This is summarized today in "21F Bolivia said NO". But such a result only marks the beginning of a new series of crimes under the political alibi of a "change process" in Bolivia.

Under these conditions and to run for reelection on October 20th, Evo Morales orders his Constitutional Court and his Supreme Electoral Tribunal to perpetrate a new prevarication with judgments and rulings that have enabled him, with the argument that "being a candidate is a human right," thus ignoring the mandate of Article 32.2 of the same American Convention on Human Rights, that they claim to apply, which mandates that "the rights of each person are limited by the rights of others, by the safety of all and by the just demands of the common good, in a democratic society." [6]

The crimes go on and on in the so-called electoral process in Bolivia, with the presence of "functional candidates" that enable the usurper candidate to sustain the farce of the regime and weaken

---

6. American Convention on Human Rights. Pact of San Jose, Costa Rica, November 7 to 22, 1969

the defense of the return to democracy, but the people struggle and prepare the "civil resistance."

The peoples of Cuba, Venezuela, Nicaragua and Bolivia are fighting against the dictatorships that oppress them, but it is not a local or national oppressor; they take on a transnational enemy, united by the objective of retaining power indefinitely as the best mechanism for impunity.

Castrochavismo as a transnational organized crime structure is a very powerful usurper with a lot of money, a lot of criminal armed forces, control of many media and many mercenaries of various specialties at its service, which has put the peoples they oppress in a true and extreme "defenseless condition."

I reiterate that the axis of confrontation today is between Democracy and Castrochavismo, or organized crime that has taken political power. It is not an ideological confrontation, it is a matter of survival in which a way of life based on freedom and justice is at stake.

If we are capable of calling things by their name and treat them accordingly, we will recover democracy and republican life more quickly in Cuba, Venezuela, Bolivia and Nicaragua and we can keep it in the rest of the countries. As long as there are dictatorships there will be no peace or security in the Americas.

2

ORGANIZED CRIME DICTATORSHIPS

CASTROIST-CHAVIST DICTATORSHIPS
ARE DELINQUENCY IN POLITICAL POWER

January 9, 2018

The Castro-Chavez alliance to recreate Castroism with Venezuelan oil and money rescued the agonizing Cuban dictatorship and birthed the Castroist-Chavist dictatorships in Venezuela, Nicaragua, and Bolivia (with Ecuador now breaking away from it). They appeared as leftist political movements for the liberation of the people. Bolivarian, socialist movements that used violence, coups d'état, and elections to finish off political parties, leaders, and democracy. A reality check now reveals that the Castroist-Chavist system is nothing more that delinquency that has seized political power.

It is vital to differentiate and separate that which is "politics" meaning an activity of public service, from that which is "organized crime" and "delinquency." Politics with its ideologies, pragmatisms, imperfections, errors, crises, even tainted by corruption is one thing, but another very different thing is politics and power under the control of associated criminals who turn politics into their main instrument for the commission of crimes, the setting up of criminal organizations, the seizure and indefinite control of power with criminal objectives and for the sake of their own impunity.

Politics in its vast meaning and according to its Greek etymology "is the art to govern or the intent to do it." It is noteworthy to point out that "in any meaning the word is used to seek one or another objective, there appears either potentially or effectively a manner

of proceeding, a practice, a series of facts, at the service of an idea."
Politics is the "art, doctrine, or opinion referring to the government
of the States", "the activities of whom govern or aspire to govern the
public affairs" and "the activities of a citizen when he or she intervenes
in public affairs."

Politics is legal, meaning that it is conducted in spheres considered
to be "just, allowed, according to justice and reason" because it is of
order and public service. Politics is totally counter to crime which is
"the guilt, the breaking of the law and all acts or omissions punished
by law." While politics takes care of "the process of making decisions
for the benefit of society", crime is all "undue and reprehensible
actions" that attempt against everything society protects and against
society itself. Politics is a public service and crime and delinquency
are a public hazard.

The objective reality shows Cuba, Venezuela, Nicaragua and
Bolivia's dictatorships continually and re-incidentally committing
all types of crime. The most severe are against life, the physical
well-being, and the freedom of the people through assassinations,
massacres, judicialized political persecution, political imprisonment,
political exile, torture and crimes against humanity that include;
hunger and misery, as control mechanisms. Financial crimes go far
beyond mere corruption because they have wrecked their productive
systems, looted state-owned enterprises, formed groups of novo-rich
or the regime's bourgeoises, taken their foreign and internal debt to
new and unpayable amounts, hocked their natural resources and the
nations' economies for decades to come.

They justify narcotics trafficking as an "instrument of their anti-
imperialist fight" as Evo Morales claims at the UN with the backing
of the rest of the dictators. Venezuela is the axis of the traffic and the
production of cocaine is controlled by the Coca Growers' Unions of
Evo Morales and the FARC from Colombia. The Cuban dictatorship

is actively involved in these crimes since the times of the Cold War, and money laundering points to Nicaragua.

There isn't a single one crime included in their criminal code the Castro's, Maduro, Ortega, Morales and their regimes have not committed, including sexual crimes, counterfeiting, kidnapping, extorsion, and coverup. The only difference with the "mafia" is that Castroist-Chavists control the political power in, at the very least, four countries.

They are not corrupted governments, they are organized delinquency that holds political power and plans to indefinitely keep holding it. These are not politicians who commit crimes, they are criminals who disguise themselves as politicians to commit crimes and hide them. They are not rulers, they are "groups of organized crime" that commit "serious crimes".

They can NO longer keep being treated as politicians, and least of all as State Dignitaries. Criminals have neither immunities, nor privileges. Their nations' sovereignty is not meant to be protection to transnational organized crime and the international community can NO longer be an accomplice.

SLAVE PHYSICIANS ARE CASTROIST-CHAVIST OCCUPATION FORCES

The sending of physicians to the world by the Cuban dictatorship under the guise of "solidarity" or "cooperation" is the application of "Castroist internationalism" that began with the guerrillas in Latin America since the sixties. The dictatorship has constituted an international political force as its greatest source of income comprised by people who have been subjugated, who are used for indoctrination, infiltration, intelligence collection, social control, mobilizations, and security, charging billions of dollars for their professional services with which it covers up its intervention. The slaved physicians are "Castroist-Chavist occupation forces".

The Cuban regime has reported that its physicians work in 62 countries and that "in 35 of them Cuba charges for the medical services rendered". The "sale of professional services", basically medical, is the main source of income reported by the Cuban dictatorship with "an estimated annual amount of $11.5 billion dollars" between 2011 and 2015. Its second source of income is the remittance of money from the United States valued at $3.3 billion dollars in 2015, and its third source is tourism which generated $2.8 billion in 2016.

Cuban physicians work with and for the regime in 24 Latin American countries and the Caribbean. Brazil, Venezuela, Bolivia, and Ecuador stand out for the number of Cuban physicians working there under the control and oversight of the Cuban regime who negotiated contracts by which Cuba is paid for services rendered and amounts from which, a small portion -estimated to be less than 25%- is given to the physicians. The Pan American Health Organization (OPS in Spanish) is the intermediary of this 21st century slaving system.

In dictatorial Cuba, to study a profession is a door to a future with views to become part of the government's structure or to be able to be free -at some point- from the oppression but at the cost of being indoctrinated and being compelled to unconditionally serve the regime. In Castroist Cuba none of the professions are free, professionals are government employees who belong to the state, to the regime, to the dictator.

Political indoctrination and military operational training are basic conditions in order to become a Cuban "internationalist". To be able to work outside of Cuba is a significant improvement compared to the island's misery, even if the regime takes the lion's share of the income generated by the individual's work which is considered "fruit of the revolution". Groups that are sent outside of Cuba are hierarchically organized, with an effective and vertical Chain of Command, with political obligations and under a permanent control. The families that are left in Cuba become a sort of hostages to ensure the good behavior of the "internationalist" members.

The arrival of Cuban physicians and other professionals, has become generalized in those Latin American countries controlled by, or under the influence of, Castroist-Chavist ideology. In Brazil with Lula and Rousseff, in Venezuela with Chavez and Maduro, in Ecuador with Correa, in Bolivia with Morales, in Chile with Bachelet, and in the "Petro-Caribbean" countries, there are thousands of Cuban physicians. Their professional skills and capabilities have been questioned, but in spite of creating conflict with their local professional counterparts, and even having some cases of mal-praxis or negligence, they have been imposed on the people under the pretext of "cooperation" for the political and operative activities they perform.

In Venezuela, Bolivia, and Nicaragua's dictatorships the political role of these "internationalist physicians" is vital for the Castroist-Chavist system. They are generally assigned to and located in poverty-stricken and rural areas with the pretext of a lack of the services they will provide and are integrated into these communities. They perform indoctrination and propaganda for the regime, they campaign against those who are identified as "enemies of change or the revolution", they also perform tasks to identify the leadership of resistance or pro-democracy groups, they recruit for and organize new political groups. They also perform reporting and intelligence tasks whenever there is conflict with operative groups

Besides being pawns of the intervention, the trans-nationalization of the anti-democratic subversion and organized crime, "Cuban internationalists" are victims of slavery, because they are forced to generate income for the dictatorship that steals from them the income from their work. Living proof are the many who have fled in Venezuela and Bolivia and the physicians' revolts in Brazil reported by the New York Times under the heading "You get tired of being a slave".

CASTROIST-CHAVIST DICTATORSHIPS MAKE UP, DIVIDE AND MANIPULATE THE OPPOSITION

The more weakened Venezuelan and Bolivian regimes are due to their spiraling crisis and their citizens' rejection, the more they need to simulate democracy forcing rigged electoral processes in order to present fraudulent victories that supplant the popular will. Given they do not have the sophistication of social control and criminal actions that the Cuban regime has to simulate elections with only one party and without any opposition, Nicolas Maduro and Evo Morales need for an opposition to exist, so they make it up, divide it, and manipulate it.

I have said it and reiterate that in Latin America's dictatorships the use of the term "political opposition" is inadequate, or -at least- inaccurate, because when there is no democracy there is no opposition but resistance and a struggle for the recouping of democracy. Political opposition is the "indispensable expression of contradiction in the democratic process of forming the political will and is co-substantial to freedom, human rights, plurality, and the alternation in power" and has as its essential feature the possibility of "getting to become the government through elections".

In democracy, the political opposition has the possibility and the right to enter into covenants with or against the government, the opposition can be diverse and plural and can be divided or united by ideological, pragmatic, or even interest issues. The freedom of expression and freedom of the press ensure the existence of democratic dynamics within a framework of respect for the law. When there is NO democracy, such as in Cuba, Venezuela, Bolivia, and Nicaragua, it is the regime that sets the conditions, the limits, the scope and even the leadership of the political opposition, take this to mean the regime "makes up its opposition" as in a cage, outside of which those admitted as opposites are not permitted to do anything.

Cuba, Venezuela, Bolivia, and Nicaragua now have regimes with the total control of power, without freedom of the press, without the separation of the branches of government and with an open manipulation of the judicial system as a mechanism for repression, political persecution, and for covering up the crimes committed by the Castro, Chavez, Maduro, Morales, and Ortega and their inner circles. This is why these are dictatorships that, furthermore, have politically persecuted, imprisoned, and exiled who are kept away -by force- from political activities within their national territory and obviously from elections and from running for office.

In a Venezuela, currently enduring a humanitarian crisis, with hundreds of political prisoners and thousands of political exiles, the illegitimate and criminal Constituent Assembly has moved up the date of elections, has disqualified candidates, and already has everything prepared for the electoral victory of the dictator Nicolas Maduro, as the candidate for the ruling party. In a Bolivia with dozens of political prisoners and over a thousand political exiles, the regime's despicable judges have chosen to ignore the referendum of 21 February 2016 (21F) and have enabled the dictator Evo Morales to, once again, be elected in 2019 and thus perpetuate himself in power.

They make up their opposition, choosing those who will be part of it and instructing them as to what they are supposed to do, with the clear understanding that whomever dares to be true opposition, risks being persecuted, jailed, exiled, or even killed. After they have made up their "opposition", they divide it by openly managing a system of rewards and punishment often expressed as financial benefits, favors, noteworthy privileges, that the people see and begin to question.

The manipulation of the opposition ranges from enabling or disabling candidates to the making of secret -but evident- covenants through which the dictatorships promote the running of other candidates, freeing political prisoners, or allowing the return of someone exiled "so that he/she be a candidate for the opposition". They deceive everyone by appearing to have several candidates for the opposition. They denounce as a "conspiracy" any effort or call to unity, as in Bolivia and when this unity is achieved, such as in the MUD's case in Venezuela, they infiltrate it, they divide it, and they disintegrate it. If any member of the opposition is able to run as a true candidate for the opposition, it has no chance.

Under those conditions no one can win an election running against the dictators; Maduro in Venezuela, Morales in Bolivia, because these really are NOT elections but "tragic comedy criminal charades" for which besides having their fraud institutionalized, they make up, divide, and manipulate their "opposition" bringing it down -through criminal Castroist-Chavist instruments and practices- to be weak hostages, accomplices or simulators that will continue to coexist with them.

WILL ECUADOR EXIT CASTROIST-CHAVIST DICTATORSHIPS' GROUP

Results from the 4 February referendum and popular consult in Ecuador reflect the unequivocal mandate of the people for the government to restore democracy. It is not an ideological matter, it is about reinstating those components that Rafael Correa and his government had suppressed, just as they did in Venezuela, Bolivia, and Nicaragua within a model that Ecuador's former President Osvaldo Hurtado had denounced as the "dictatorships of the 21st century socialism". Ecuador's current president Lenin Moreno is stronger but there is doubt whether he wants and is able to remove Ecuador from the Castroist-Chavist dictatorships' group.

Let us remember that "Castroist-Chavist" is the label for "Fidel Castro and Hugo Chavez's undertaking that, using the subversive capabilities of the Cuban dictatorial regime and Venezuelan oil, had resurrected -commencing in 1999- the expansion of Castroist, antidemocratic communism with a heavy antiimperialist discourse." With lots of funds and lots of crime, it was spread through the region to the point that -at its peak- it controlled the majority of member states from the Organization of American States (OAS) and the OAS itself. The Castroist-Chavist system is now in crisis, yet it still controls Cuba, Venezuela, Bolivia, and Nicaragua and has influence over the Petro-Caribbean countries. There are signs, however, that Ecuador may exit from this group.

When Rafael Correa got to power and was elected President of Ecuador on 15 January of 2007, he subjected his country under the Caracas-Havana axis. Components of democracy gradually disappeared through; the institutionalized violation of human rights and individual freedoms, his total control of the branches of government, his misuse of the judicial branch as a means for repression, political persecution, and seizure, the disappearance of the "Rule of Law", the existence of political persecutions, imprisonments, and exiles, as well as his total control of mass media, and the annulment of the freedom of the press. Correa institutionalized electoral fraud, openly supported narco-terrorist groups, such as the FARC, eliminated public control and allowed corruption to be widespread; abused indigenous natives and their territories, misappropriated national resources, and called for his indefinite reelection and more.

On 24 May of 2017, Correa left the government in the hands of his "dolphin" acolyte Lenin Moreno. An Ecuadorean nation in economic crisis, overly in debt, without a clear determination of the amount, with politically persecuted, imprisoned, and exiles, with denouncements of electoral fraud, and the deliberate coverup of corruption, and with unprecedented impunity, without freedom of the press, discharging his duties in the typical fashion of a Castroist-Chavist dictatorship. It was, perhaps, this shameful and bitter reality that made Lenin Moreno to challenge himself to truly be the president of Ecuador instead of being the successor and concealer of Rafael Correa's dictatorship, and to seek change through the referendum and popular consult.

Now that Lenin Moreno's political standing has been boosted and he has received the people's mandate -which has surpassed the two-thirds of votes in average- to restore democracy in Ecuador, the question remains as to whether he wants it and is able to do it. The question also remains as to whether the political circles of the Post-Correa regime will allow this to happen and whether or not Moreno will be neutralized by the international threat of the Castroist-Chavist system. Moreno's discourse is interesting but members of his government do not take action and as a result his relationship with the dictatorships keep him under suspicion and his foreign policy continues to be that of Correa.

This is not an ideological matter because neither Lenin Moreno, nor his government, nor anyone need to stop being leftists, or progressives, in order to be democratic and fulfill the intent of the Interamerican Democratic Charter, the Universal Declaration of Human Rights, and the Constitution. It is neither a rightist nor a leftist thing to return under the Rule of Law, to respect the separation and independence of the branches of government, to free political prisoners, to cease persecutions, to promote the return of exiles, to respect the freedom of the press.

It is neither an ideological matter to remove Ecuador from the ever-shrinking group of governments concealing their dictatorship in Cuba, Venezuela, Bolivia, and Nicaragua. The dictatorships of the Castro's in Cuba, Nicolas Maduro in Venezuela, Evo Morales in Bolivia, and the Ortega's in Nicaragua represent narcotics trafficking, terrorism, forced migration, exile, crisis, control of power by organized thugs and that is definitely NOT politics, it is organized crime. When we deal with crime, there are no rightists or leftists, only criminals and President Lenin Moreno now has the opportunity of not remaining trapped by the Castroist-Chavist criminal plot.

A NEW ERA OF ZERO TOLERANCE
TO DICTATORSHIPS IN THE AMERICAS

The humanitarian crisis to which the Castroist-Chavist dictatorship has taken the people from Venezuela is compelling the region's and world's governments to reflect on the importance to defend democracy. The accelerated and ruthless process to consolidate Maduro's dictatorship has turned it into something undesirable, into something to be condemned, into something that is a threat to international peace and security. Only the regimes from Cuba, Bolivia, Nicaragua, and Ecuador defend Maduro, while a new era of zero tolerance for dictatorships in the Americas gains strength.

Up to now in this century, but above it all after the drafting of the Interamerican Democratic Charter (Lima-Peru 11 September of 2001) most of the region's governments allowed, assisted, or participated in the formation of 21st Century Socialism or Castroist-Chavist dictatorships. Some by deed and some by omission, but almost all under the irresistible pressure of Venezuelan resources misappropriated by Hugo Chavez, the dealings of the Forum of Sao Paolo now unraveled through the Brazilian lava jato scandal, or the threat and fear machinations of Fidel Castro and his renewed capability to destabilize governments using Venezuela's resources.

They toppled the governments of Argentina (2001), Bolivia (2003), Ecuador (2000 and 2005), and that of the OAS' General Secretary (2004) and grossly misrepresented these as resignations, converted the Cuban dictatorship as a political reference, and then recognized it as having regional leadership. In the ten years of Insulza as the Secretary General, they allowed the shameful violation of the objectives and principles of the OAS to take place under pressure from Chavez and Castro.

They let themselves to be seduced or to be compelled to accept an organized crime system that has replaced politics, controlling power in Cuba with the Castro's, in Venezuela with Chavez and Maduro, in Bolivia with Evo Morales, in Nicaragua with the Ortega's, and it appears still yet in Ecuador with the Correa scheme, and influencing the small Caribbean or Petro-Caribe countries with oil handouts.

What is happening in Venezuela today is the result of almost two decades of progressive and sustained abuses to freedom and democracy, violation of human rights, persecutions, electoral fraud, corruption, violation of the sovereignty of the country, embezzlement and misappropriation of the nation's resources, theft of government and private resources, institutional supplanting, assassinations, massacres, killing of the freedom of the press, elimination of the Rule of Law, disappearance of the separation and independence of the branches of government, control of the opposition, political prisoners and exiles, narcotics trafficking and all that may be necessary to make Venezuela a Castroist dictatorial "narco-state with a humanitarian crisis".

Ignoring times and distances, it would appear that Cuba's history of the sixties is being repeated. The dictatorship must be consolidated and therefore it; jails, represses, kills people, it generates a famine, and through fear and insecurity it causes the forced migration of those citizens that could have defied them. The thing here is that we are in the midst of the 21st century with a vast technology and communications' evolution, with the internet, social media, and citizens' reporting in real time, that show the criminal and anti-national nature of the dictatorship that now oppresses Venezuelans. Compared to the Cuba of the sixties, the ideological falsehood, the liberation pretext, and the anti-imperialistic rhetoric are no longer convincing.

It is for the aforementioned reasons that Venezuela's dictator Maduro has very few probabilities to sustain himself in the illegitimate power he holds. The international democratic community has understood that for the sake of their own interests and security, it must preclude Venezuela from turning into the second consolidated dictatorship of the Americas, and prevent the dictatorships of Bolivia and Nicaragua from following that path. Liberating Venezuela soon is a strategic necessity.

Castro's dictatorship in Cuba has subjugated its people to a permanent humanitarian crisis, but now knows that will not be tolerated any longer. Evo Morales' dictatorship has turned Bolivia into another narco-state who lags just a couple of chapters behind Venezuela's script of crime and crisis. The Ortega's dictatorship in Nicaragua with a model pro-bourgeoisie more along the lines of Somoza than Castro, has been uncovered. It has become clearer than ever that we have "two Americas", one that is democratic and the other that is dictatorial, and those two Americas cannot co-exist. Now is the era of zero tolerance to dictatorships in the Americas.

NARCO-STATES AND VENEZUELA AND BOLIVIA'S ANTI-IMPERIALIST DICTATORS

The ending of democracy and the onset of dictatorships with a populist disguise in Venezuela, Bolivia, Nicaragua, and Correa's Ecuador, as well as the threat looming over Colombia to be Cuba's operational satellite, all have as an essential component the control of political power to pursue narcotics trafficking that they all seek to cover up with their anti-imperialist discourse against the United States. For the Castroist Chavist system, narcotics' trafficking is key in its strategy, something we cannot afford to ignore in the fight to restore democracy in narco-states with self-proclaimed anti-imperialist dictators such as in Venezuela, Bolivia, and others still under cover.

History shows isolated cases of partial takeover of power by narcotics' traffickers, or cases of temporary control through political candidates or legislators in Colombia, or the case of dictator Noriega in Panama. Up to the time of the alliance between Hugo Chavez and Fidel Castro that birthed the so called, Bolivarian movement, 21st Century Socialism, or simply "Castroist Chavist" doctrine, however, we had never seen the simultaneous total control of several countries wherefrom all types of narcotics' trafficking crimes are committed and who are internationally defended.

The neo-logism title of "narco-state" describes "those countries whose political institutions are significantly influenced by narcotics' trafficking and whose leadership are government officials who are, at the same time, members of drug production or trafficking networks shielding themselves behind their legal privileged status in order to pursue criminal activities". News media, international representatives, academic experts, and even the evidence of judicial rulings, all render Venezuela with Nicolas Maduro and Bolivia with Evo Morales the status of narco-states.

Some of the proof in Venezuela's case are the nephews of Maduro's wife condemned in New York for narcotics' trafficking, or the rescue efforts to avoid the extradition from Aruba to the US of General "Pollo Carvajal" former intelligence chief of the regime. Today, Venezuela is known as "the narcotics' axis" of cocaine from the Colombian FARC with an official trafficking route from Bolivian territory controlled by Evo Morales.

In Bolivia, the top and perpetual leader of the coca leaf harvesters, Evo Morales, is the head of the Plurinational State of Bolivia wherein "by decree of law" he has increased the lawful cultivation of coca by 83% from 12,000 to 22,000 hectares and has increase the cultivation of unlawful coca from the existing 3,000 hectares in 2003 –the year they toppled President Sanchez de Lozada- to the current 50,000 hectares. The coca leaf harvesters' unions from the tropical areas of Cochabamba are his main political base for mobilizations and repression, as seen in the massacre of Cochabamba on 11 January of 2007. Morales' coca leaf harvesters –under the protection from the State- have now become cocaine producers.

Senator Roger Pinto, recently deceased in an "aviation accident" currently under investigation in Brazil, was persecuted, forced to seek asylum in the Brazilian embassy in La Paz, and afterwards exiled for publicly denouncing the link of official flights with cargo loads of drugs from Bolivia to Venezuela. Evo Morales' drug czar Colonel Rene Sanabria was arrested by DEA for cocaine trafficking and has been sentenced by US judges to jail, where he is now serving time.

Both, Venezuela's and Bolivia's regimes have expelled the US DEA from their country. DEA conducted intelligence gathering and international coordination tasks with excellent results in the fight against narcotics' trafficking. These regimes have also expelled the accredited US Ambassadors to their country. Following the same pro-narcotics policy disguised as anti-imperialism, Rafael Correa in Ecuador expelled the DEA, the US Ambassador, and removed all US presence from the US counternarcotics base at Manta in Guayaquil, Ecuador.

Narco-states, moreover, make the defense of their illicit activities a matter of international policy. Evo Morales in his address to the UN –with the backing of Cuba, Venezuela, Ecuador, Nicaragua- has requested the decriminalization of drug production, has accused DEA for Morales' own crimes (as he is accustomed to do), and has proclaimed that *"the fight against narcotics' trafficking is an instrument of imperialism"*.

Brazil, Argentina, and Chile now flooded by drugs from Bolivia have started to take action, the government of Colombia now reacts against Venezuela's dictatorship, Ecuador appears to be leaving the group of narco-states and the US Ambassador to the UN, Nikky Haley, has described "Venezuela as a violent narco-state who is a threat to the world".

TO DIFFERENTIATE AND SEPARATE POLITICS FROM ORGANIZED CRIME

Americas' reality worsens because the Castroist Chavist system has shown us that its actions and objectives are not a matter of politics but are entirely a matter of organized crime. The division between countries with democracy and those with dictatorships is no longer enough. The regimes from Cuba, Venezuela, Bolivia, Nicaragua, and Correa's Ecuador besides having established de-facto governments concentrating all power and being sustained by violence, are deeply involved in transnational organized crime. We, therefore, must differentiate and separate politics from organized crime, calling it by what they really are.

The Palermo convention which includes Cuba, Venezuela, Bolivia, Nicaragua, Ecuador, and all Americas' countries defines "an organized criminal group" to be "a structured group of three or more persons that may exist during a certain time and who deliberately acts with the purpose of committing one or more serious crimes or crimes catalogued by this Convention which are aimed to obtain, directly or indirectly, an economic or some other material benefit." The Castro, Chavez-Maduro, Morales, Ortega, and Correa's regimes are certainly included in the aforementioned definition.

The Convention defines "serious crime" as "the conduct which entails a crime punishable with a maximum of four years imprisonment or harsher sentence". The Castroist Chavist chieftains have committed all sorts of serious crimes and as evidence that they are habitual and repeat offenders, let's take a look at some of these crimes; attempts against life and liberty, assassinations, undue detentions, torture, crimes against the economies of their states, corruption, counterfeiting of all sorts, supplanting authority, usurpation of power, depriving people their rights, treason to their homeland, aggravated robbery, heists, kidnappings, extortion, narcotics' trafficking, conspiracy, criminal cover up, human trafficking, contraband, terrorism, and other common crimes against humanity.

A "structured group" is "a group which has not been fortuitously formed for the immediate commission of a crime and in which roles, outlined in functional descriptions formally defined, are not necessarily assigned to the members who comprise it and wherein there may not be continuity for its members or there is no structure developed". In the case of Cuba, Venezuela, Bolivia, and Nicaragua, the "structured group" definition is certainly applicable because in the Castroist Chavist system there is assignment of functions and its has a well developed and institutionalized structure in the governments under its control.

For "assets, we shall understand to mean any type of asset; material, real estate, tangible, or intangible, and the documents or legal means which accredit the ownership or any other right over such assets." By "product of the crime, we shall understand to include any type of asset obtained, directly or indirectly, through the commission of a crime". Thus we now have a clear picture showing that *the main asset, product of a crime by a structured criminal group who started as "the Bolivarian Movement", "21st Century Socialism", and now "Castroist Chavist" system "is to exercise and illegitimately retain power" and through the indefinite hold of power continue to commit and cover up all types of crime.*

It has spread from Cuba, and now controls Venezuela, Bolivia, and Nicaragua. It functions as a transnational organization and presents itself as a political undertaking with a leftist, populist, socialist, communist –whichever best suits it- ideology. With the resources gotten from crime, it controls and influences the news media, powerful lobby groups, attorneys, public relations firms, personalities, institutions, and even governments in order to sustain the appearance of a political undertaking to disguise what in reality is an unprecedented criminal organization.

With "the product of the crime" it controls and/or influences international organizations such as; Petrocaribe, the Organization of American States (OAS), the United Nations (UN), and it forges alliances with anti-democratic governments, jostling and negotiating positions wherefrom, instead of protecting the system they misuse it and place it at its service to protect narcotics' trafficking, terrorism, and all sorts of crime it commits daily in order to indefinitely sustain itself in power.

The greatest threat against democracy, peace, and international security in the Americas is organized crime which controls Cuba, Venezuela, Bolivia, and Nicaragua. Ecuador is now, perhaps, on its way out of this scheme. Democratic governments must clearly understand to separate politics from organized crime and act accordingly and for the sake of their own security because the peril is so great that whoever did not understand this is now imprisoned, exiled, or dead.

DICTATORS AND ORGANIZED CRIME IN LIMA'S SUMMIT OF THE AMERICAS

"Democratic governance against corruption" is the main theme of the eighth Summit of the Americas (10-14 April, Lima, Peru) in a region divided into "two Americas" between those countries with democracy and dictatorial regimes of organized crime. None of the essential components of democracy are respected in Cuba, Venezuela, Bolivia, and Nicaragua whose presidents have corruption and impunity as their objective in order to remain indefinitely in power. This fragile context is the challenge for democratic leaders of the Americas who need to be different than the organized crime chieftains.

The Organization of American States (OAS) has, as its basis, the Interamerican Democratic Charter through which it spells out that "the essential components of democracy are, amongst others; respect for human rights and basic freedoms, access to and exercise of power subject to the Rule of Law, the conduct of elections periodically, free, fair, and based on the universal and secret suffrage as an expression of the people's sovereignty; a plural regime of multiple political parties and organizations, and the separation and independence of the branches of government.

The Summit of the Americas "are periodic meetings that gather Heads of State and governments democratically elected to debate and make decisions on the region's relevant matters". They are conceived "to debate on shared political concerns, to affirm common values and commit to coordinated actions at the local and regional levels in order to confront present and future challenges facing the nations of the Americas.

Governance, according to the OAS means "institutional stability and effectiveness in decision making and management. . ." The PNUD focuses "democratic governance" as "the challenge to create institutions and processes that better respond to the needs of ordinary citizens, including the poor", seeking "to foster the participation, the responsibility, and the effectiveness at all levels."

This framework of principles and institutionalism enables us to differentiate that which is corruption as a crime and a political act in a democracy from that which is corruption as an essential component of non-democratic regimes that have made power to be an instrument of Transnational Organized Crime, as defined by the "Palermo Convention."

In a democracy, corruption is not the rule but the flaw, it is the violation of normalcy, "the misuse of governmental power to get illegitimate advantages, generally in a secret or private way", it is "the consistent practice of utilizing the functions and means of the government for the benefit –whether this benefit be financial or otherwise- of those who are involved in it." In a democracy, there are investigations, prosecution, and punishment with accountability, there is separation and independence of the branches of government, the Rule of Law exists, and there is freedom of the press. On the other hand, however, in dictatorships, corruption is the means, the cause, and the end objective of getting to, and indefinitely remaining in power.

The better democracy is, the more control and punishment of corruption there is, because there is freedom and transparency as shown by Peru, Brazil, Chile, Costa Rica, the United States in their dealing with the "Lava Jato" scandal or the transnational organized corruption of the Forum of Sao Paolo with Odebrecht and the other construction companies. The flip side of that, in the dictatorships of Cuba, Venezuela, Bolivia, Nicaragua, and Ecuador/Correa, there is concealment, cover-up, and impunity.

The designator as Regimes with Organized Crime to Cuba, Venezuela, Bolivia, and Nicaragua is owed to crimes that go far beyond corruption in their governmental contracts. It is due to crimes against life, perpetrated through institutionalized violence, massacres, and humanitarian crises; crimes against freedom with political persecutions, jailing, political exiles and forced migrations, narcotics trafficking with narco-states as Venezuela and Bolivia are now known as. It is for crimes against the state's security, such as; terrorism and the existence of irregular armed groups. It is for crimes against the national estate or patrimony, and other crimes stemming from the illegitimate and illegal holding of power.

The main theme of Lima's Summit of the Americas is; what will democratic governments do against the organized crime instilled in the political power of Cuba, Venezuela, Bolivia, and Nicaragua? Maduro, the dictator, has not been invited to attend but his creator and mentor Raul Castro from Cuba and his partners Evo Morales from Bolivia, and Ortega from Nicaragua call for him to attend, and undoubtedly will represent him.

MAKE-BELIEVE OPPOSITION IN ORGANIZED CRIME DICTATORSHIPS

The farce staged by Dictator Nicolas Maduro to manipulate elections in Venezuela and perpetuate himself in power has revealed a make-believe opposition as another of the dictatorship's fundamental components in the Americas. In their quest to appear democratic they need to have an opposition and they implement it with accomplice operators that contribute to the sustainment of the regime. This make-believe opposition is at work in Venezuela, Bolivia, and Nicaragua to sustain organized crime's dictatorships.

There is neither democracy, nor valid elections, in regimes that manipulate the ballots with a single party system that is forced or otherwise imposed upon the people, as in Cuba. In the Castroist expansion of the 21stCentury, the dictatorships chose to utilize democracy in order to supplant institutionalism and eliminate essential components of democracy. They used the people's votes to commit fraud, they supplanted their constitutions and replaced their institutional structure with dictatorial statutes which are proof in and by themselves that there is no democracy.

Under the direction of Cuba; Venezuela with Hugo Chavez and Nicolas Maduro, Bolivia with Evo Morales, Nicaragua with Daniel Ortega, and at one time Ecuador with Rafael Correa, conducted frequent elections and in order to win them, they staged a system of apparently credible simulators. Part of the fraud and make-believe actions implemented by the dictatorships of the 21stCentury Socialism, now turned into Organized Crime's dictatorships was and is the creation, domestication, and manipulation of a "make-believe opposition".

The political and social actors in Venezuela, Bolivia, and Nicaragua are the make-believe opposition to the regime that appear, feign, and mimic to be true oppositors when, in reality, they are hard at work to sustain it. They introduce themselves as oppositors, promise changes, propose to win elections to give back to the people their freedom, but in reality they are playing along to indefinitely perpetuate their dictators in power. This make-believe opposition is an essential part of the fraud, deception to the people and the international community. The simulated opposition is, simply stated; fraud, entrapment, rigging, and is part of the crime that Organized Crime's regimes become institutionalized with a façade of normalcy in order to hold on to power.

The most noteworthy case, at this time, is that of the candidate presented as the opposition's candidate in the forthcoming elections that the dictatorship has orchestrated illegally and lacking legitimacy in Venezuela. The whole world knows this to be part of the rigging of the process, rigged to ensure Nicolas Maduro is perpetuated in power. It is the calling to elections by a de-facto Constituent Assembly that functions usurping power in order to sustain the dictatorship in a country turned into a narco-state. We must insist, this is a criminal act that makes both; the dictatorial regime, as well as the make-believe opposition, responsible.

Sadly enough, the existence of make-believe opposition to benefit and sustain Organized Crime's dictatorships, doesn't only apply to Venezuela, but has spread into Bolivia and Nicaragua where there are very small pockets of true civic and political resistance, and where the opposition has no chance of accessing to power through clean and fair elections, and where leaders of the true opposition are now political prisoners or exiles.

We now endure the utilization of a "make-believe" opposition in Venezuela and it is urgent to denounce it so that the world know that the coming 20 May elections is nothing but the Venezuelan Castroist Chavist dictatorship's orchestration to ensure their anticipated outcome through the use of a make-believe opposition. To demonstrate true opposition in this charade is very simple and it consists of all political and civic organizations to refuse to participate in such a criminal proceeding.

The next scenario, one in which a make-believe opposition is already hard at work, is happening in Bolivia where Evo Morales was deemed unable to run again as a candidate in elections of 2019. He was disqualified by a popular mandate through a referendum on 21 February of 2016 (21F). Morales is now conducting electoral campaigns and "opposition" candidates are now surfacing with a clear mandate to multiply and in the process divide the popular rejection expressed by the 21F referendum, and deceive Bolivians by convincing them that the "opposition" has a chance to defeat the dictator. The names of those Bolivian make-believe oppositors are already on the news media, some self-promoted, some others promoted and endorsed by their constituents, but all staging a charade so that Bolivians ignore that NO means NO and to keep this fraudulent electoral charade of Organized Crime from falling apart.

VENEZUELA, THE GORDIAN KNOT OF ORGANIZED CRIME'S DICTATORSHIPS

Hugo Chavez and Nicolás Maduro's dictatorship in Venezuela is the origin and support of all dictatorships in the Americas. Without the Venezuelan oil, the expansion of Castroist doctrine in the 21stCentury would not have happened, but nowadays its sustainment is not possible without the Transnational Organized Crime from the Venezuelan narco-state. If the Venezuelan dictatorship falls, the dictatorships of Cuba, Bolivia, and Nicaragua will fall apart. The Gordian knot of the Organized Crime's dictatorships of the Americas is the Venezuelan regime and following years of attempts to unknot it, it is now time to cut it.

The term "Gordian Knot" comes from the Greek legend of "Gordias", a farmer from Frigia in the region we now know as Turkey who, after he was elected King offered his cart tying the spear and the yoke with "a knot whose ends were hidden on the inside, so complicated that no one was able to unknot it" with the omen that "whoever unknots the knot would conquer the whole of Asia". When Alexander the Great conquered Frigia they challenged him to unknot the Gordian knot and taking his sword he cut it instead, solving this way the prolonged matter, the source of the expression "to cut is just as good as to unknot it" claimed by King Fernando the Catholic as his logo in his coat of arms.

The "Gordian knot" is "a very entangled knot or impossible to unknot", "an indissoluble difficulty", a "difficult obstacle to get over or one with a difficult solution", "to be solved bluntly and without second thoughts". It refers to the kind of difficulty that takes a long time to solve, causes many complications due to the lack of a solution and one that needs creative, decisive, but very intelligent, solutions.

The Venezuelan dictatorship is the Gordian knot that keeps the Venezuelan people from recovering their freedom and democracy, one that at the same time sustains dictatorships in the Americas, specifically in Cuba, Bolivia, and Nicaragua as a system of Transnational Organized Crime and a real danger not only for this region, but the whole world.

Up to now, in the 21st Century, the Venezuelan people has done just about everything. It tried to believe in the proclaimed good intentions of Hugo Chavez that turned out to be vile lies. It tried to stop the dictatorial oppression through the ballots and elections wherein victory meant nothing. It sacrificed the freedom and the lives of thousands of Venezuelans massacred, assassinated, tortured, imprisoned, persecuted and exiled. It believed in a political leadership who it empowered with electoral victories such as the one from the National Assembly, without any results. It took to the streets with massive demonstrations that were brutally repressed. It is victim of a humanitarian crisis, but it continues to fight.

The Gordian knot of the Organized Crime dictatorship in Venezuela has not been unknotted. Orchestrated by Cuba's Castroists with alliances of spurious interests of states tied to terrorism and Transnational Organized Crime who utilize Venezuela as a political and geographic base in their aggression to the United States and western Civilization.

The problem of Venezuela's dictatorship -the expansion of Cuba's dictatorship that also controls Bolivia and Nicaragua- is not of a political or ideological nature, because it is not a confrontation of the left with the right, or of socialism against capitalism, and is not only of abusive holders of power against their victims. It is the Transnational Organized Crime who controls several states -the knot is Venezuela- to commit crime against humanity, massacres, tortures, jailing, narcotics' trafficking, terrorism, and much more, committed with impunity and under the guise of sovereignty, to establish geopolitical bases against international peace and security in the hemisphere.

It is a real and current threat for all the region's democratic countries. The hundreds of thousands of forced migrants already impact the economy, security, and stability of, practically, all the Americas' free countries such as; Brazil, Colombia, Panama, Peru, Chile, the United States, Mexico. The hub of narcotics' trafficking that Venezuela has been turned into, with the Colombian FARC's cocaine and with Evo Morales' coca growers' unions from Bolivia, has penetrated the entire region and impacts the whole world with serious consequences in security and the wellbeing of the people.

Venezuela's Gordian knot has not been unknotted, it is now time to do just as Alexander the Great did, cut it. The cut with intelligence and speed is needed, for the sake of all of Americas' democratic countries' interests.

PEOPLE UNMASK ORGANIZED CRIME'S DICTATORSHIP IN NICARAGUA

May 1, 2018

Nicaragua has gone past the point of no return for the recovery of its freedom and democracy. The repressed citizens' protests, the Castroist Chavist modus operandi already applied by Chavez and Maduro in Venezuela and by Evo Morales in Bolivia with several dead and wounded, have unmasked a shameful governmental system the Nicaraguans are not willing to continue to tolerate. The issue now is Daniel Ortega's departure and the end of his regime, because the people have unmasked the Organized Crime's dictatorship in Nicaragua.

Amongst Cuba, Venezuela, Bolivia, and Nicaragua, the four states that still remain under the control of Organized Crime's dictatorships, Nicaragua appeared to be the most stable or controlled. Ortega's agreements to cover up the political corruption of his former adversaries, then turned into his collaborators and accomplices, were the essential cornerstone to establish the Castroist Chavist model for simulating democracy in Nicaragua and for quickly establishing it as one of the fastest growing dictatorship of the 21stCentury Socialism. Arrangements with private business owners along with granted privileges and perks, were the protection mechanism to the dictatorship's façade.

Venezuelan resources and oil misappropriated by Hugo Chavez, enabled Daniel Ortega's administration to appear to be prosperous when, in reality, the foundation was being laid in for an Organized Crime's system – a feature of non-democratic regimes- to be established there. These non-democratic regimes started presenting themselves as populist, leftist, pro-Castroist, and ended up as a dangerous Transnational Organized Crime's group.

Nicaragua's regime labored hard to keep itself with a low profile while the Americas and the world were pointing to Cuba, Venezuela, and Bolivia as dictatorships. But now the Ortega's Nicaragua is on the headlines and is being included -with no differences- as part of the group of its partners; the Castro's, Maduro, and Morales. It is being included in the group that commits and covers up all sorts of crimes against humanity, violates human rights, persecutes, exiles, assassinates, massacres, counterfeits, extorts, and sustains terrorism, as narco-states in order to hold on to power at all cost as a means to remain unpunished.

What started out as a complaint against reforms to the Social Security Institute imposed by the Ortega's in Nicaragua, has turned into a heated general protest for all of the affront suffered and endured by the Nicaraguan people who now see the ending of the regime, the departure of Daniel Ortega and his organization from the government, as the only solution. Reality shows that there isn't one single citizen, none of the different sectors, that has not been a victim of the regime. It shows that it censored, controlled, and repressed the press, imposed mandatory membership in the government's ruling party in order to qualify for, or remain in, a government job, eliminated the opposition from the electoral process, controlled the judicial branch in order to use it with "despicable rulings" against adversaries or defenders of freedom, and formed a new cast of novo rich with the resources from the State, corruption and crime.

It has been a long time that in Nicaragua there isn't any of the essential components of democracy. There is no freedom, no respect for Human Rights, there is no Rule of Law, there is no division or independence of the branches of government, there are no free and fair elections and the universal suffrage has been supplanted, there is no freedom of political organization. It has been years that valiant Nicaraguans denounce to the world the Ortega's dictatorship. It has been years that the people have been shouting that "Somoza and Ortega are the same thing".

A well-orchestrated international system of public relations (PR), lobbyists who work for the Cuba-Venezuela-Bolivia-Nicaragua group, the subjecting of Petro Caribe countries with bribes of Venezuelan oil, its penetration into international organizations, its control over the national news media and its creation and influence over international media, its collusion with important magnates and businessmen, and its repetitive anti-US discourse along with its opening to Russia, China, North Korea, and Iran, have all been factors -among others- that have allowed the existence of the Ortega's Organized Crime's dictatorship in Nicaragua.

Today we are in one other scenario. The people from Nicaragua with their heroism, courage, and persistence have unmasked the dictatorship that controls their country and they have presented it to the world for what it really is; a group of organized crime that must leave from power as soon as possible to give way to democracy.

IN CUBA, VENEZUELA, BOLIVIA, AND NICARAGUA, THERE IS NO FREEDOM OF THE PRESS

May 16, 2018

When holders of political power end freedom of the press, they have closed the circle of oppression, there is no longer any of the essential components of democracy in existence. There is no half-way freedom of the press. Freedom of the press is the last bastion of defense of freedom and democracy. In the mold of the Organized Crime's dictatorships, the control and manipulation of the news media is the main instrument used for the sustainment of the regime, as it is now happening in Cuba, Venezuela, Bolivia, and Nicaragua.

Freedom of the press is a right. The basis for freedom of the press as a right is included in Article 19 of the Universal Declaration for Human Rights, which states; *"Every individual has the right to have freedom of opinion and of expression; this right includes not to be harassed due to the individual's opinion and expression, it includes to be able to investigate, and receive, information and opinions, and to broadcast them, without limitation of borders, by any means of expression."*

The UNESCO considers freedom of the press as "a main component of the greater right of freedom of expression". There is freedom of the press when "citizens can exercise their right to edit the means of communication whose content is neither controlled, nor censured by the branches of government". Freedom of the press is the right to investigate and inform without any kind of coercion or threats, such as; prior censorship, harassment, or any act aimed at altering or annulling the will.

Freedom of the press is guaranteed by the "respect to Human Rights and basic civil liberties", by the existence of the "Rule of Law", by the "separation and independence of the branches of government", which along with the "celebration of periodic, free and fair elections based on the universal and secret suffrage as an expression of the people's sovereignty" and a regime of plurality of political parties and organizations, constitute the fundamental components of democracy. Freedom of the press is inherent to democracy, it needs the conditions from democracy to exist while, at the same time, it guarantees them.

The 21st Century in the Americas has demonstrated that the model of the alliance between Castro and Chavez imposed its methodology of violation of human rights and basic civic liberties, it took control of all branches of the government, eliminated the Rule of Law, supplanted existing constitutions, imposed "despicable laws" violating human rights, institutionalized electoral fraud, persecuted, jailed, and exiled anyone opposing them thus destroying the system of plurality of political parties and organizations. When the now dictators from Venezuela, Bolivia, and Nicaragua, using the Cuban model, controlled all branches of government and supplanted the Rule of Law, they attacked and ended the free press.

Cuba with the Castro's, Venezuela with Chavez and Maduro, Bolivia with Evo Morales, Nicaragua with Daniel Ortega, and Ecuador with Rafael Correa, replaced freedom of the press with a system of control of the information with prior censorship, self-censorship, financial and judicial repression. They appropriated themselves -through transfers under duress, seizures, intervention, and violence- of private news media in order to place them at their service, they have supported and created state media, founded and funded regional media, they manage the official propaganda as a mechanism for extorsion, they use taxes as a means of pressure and retribution, they extort companies regarding the assignment of their propaganda, they start and sustain "assassination of reputation" campaigns against journalists and owners of news media.

Attacks, aggression, disappearances, and assassinations have been portrayed as common crime, when there are police complaint reports and well-founded suspicion that these were crimes aimed to specifically silence the freedom of the press. Several journalists and news media businessmen are in exile, many more are unemployed, harassed, and prosecuted. Others, subjugated by either fear or need to the shamefulness of the regime.

In the absence of democracy and the existence of Organized Crime's dictatorships in Cuba, Venezuela, Bolivia, and Nicaragua, we can no longer continue treating the issue of freedom of the press in relative terms. Objective reality does not allow us to think there is a little bit of freedom, or that a bit of it still remains. The facts show there is no freedom of the press simply and solely because there are no conditions of democracy there.

POLITICAL PRISONERS OF THE
ORGANIZED CRIME'S REGIMES

May 31, 2018

There are hundreds of political prisoners in the Americas. They are the victims of another series of crimes committed -under a transnational mold- by those who govern Cuba, Venezuela, Bolivia, Nicaragua, Ecuador/Correa, and Argentina/Kirchner to deprive citizens who have been earmarked as a "political threat" of their freedom, to retaliate, or set a precedent to instill fear. The 21st Century Socialism's political prisoners are falsely accused of common crimes and the government manipulates the justice system as a means of political persecution and control, applying "despicable laws" and rulings. Political prisoners are Transnational Organized Crime's prisoners.

Political prisoner is "the physical person that is kept in jail or has been detained some other way because his ideas suppose a challenge or a threat to the established political system". It is about people who are considered a "political threat" and who are deprived of their freedom without the existence of any real legal reasons, in violation of their human rights and by the government's arbitrary decision, with accusations levied and prosecution executed simulating a legal due process.

The Venezuelan "Penal Forum" a Non-Governmental Organization "to assist victims of human rights' violations" describes three categories of political prisoners; "**Category 1**; those people detained or condemned for representing, individually, a political threat to the government because they are social or political leaders. In these cases, the purpose of their detention is to exclude the individual from political activities, neutralize the individual as a factor of social or political mobilization, isolating the person from the rest of the population. **Category 2**; those people detained or condemned, not because they represent an individual political threat to the regime, but because they are part of a social group that needs to be intimidated. Those who stand out in this group are; students, social and political activists, among others. **Category 3**; those people who are neither considered an individual political threat, nor are members of a social group considered a threat but are used by the government to sustain a government's campaign or a determined political narrative dealing with certain important situations of national significance."

The common main feature of political prisoners of the regimes installed by the Havana-Caracas' axis in the 21stCentury, is the misuse of the judicial branch. It is the misuse of the justice system to accuse, investigate, detain, or justify future detentions, initiate judicial prosecution, produce despicable rulings and sentences, and institute a brutal penitentiary system under the slogan "there are no political prisoners but politicians who are prisoners".

Cuba's judicial system is the totalitarian regime's part that has the function of protecting the regime itself instead of administering justice. This feature has been the mold for Hugo Chavez and Nicolas Maduro in Venezuela Rafael Correa in Ecuador, Daniel Ortega in Nicaragua, Evo Morales in Bolivia, the Kirchner's in Argentina to establish a system of their own comprised by "the regime's prosecutors and judges" who are backed by "despicable laws/rulings" in order to disguise and misrepresent political persecutions as common crime cases.

"Despicable Law" is the norm that has been drafted and established in compliance with formal legal procedures for its creation but that violates in content and purpose Human Rights and fundamental civil liberties". These are laws the Castroist Chavist regimes approve due to the control they have over the Legislative Branch of their government and sustain them with the control they have over the constitutionality of things and who enforce them with the control they have over the regime's prosecutors and judges.

The common content, among others, of "despicable laws" used in Cuba, Venezuela, Ecuador/Correa, Bolivia, Nicaragua and Argentina/ Kirchner are; to annul the retroactivity of the law that is a human right, pass gag laws, modify the Penal Codes, worsen sentences and new crimes, investigate facts with new despicable laws over matters already prescribed, abolish and repeal existing laws, eliminate guarantees for the performance of attorney's responsibilities. Subject people to a defenseless situation, "assassinate someone's reputation" through control over the news media, intimidate, accuse, and imprison attorneys who defend cases, persecute prosecutors and judges who are no longer willing to execute the government's atrocities or those who describe and prove beyond doubt -with recurrence and re-incidence- crimes committed by the Castro's, Chavez, Maduro, Correa, Ortega, Morales, Kirchner and their inner circles, confessed by the same prosecutors and judges who fled the Organized Crime's system they formerly served, and by the hundreds of victims who are in jail or with home-arrest.

ORGANIZED CRIME REGIMES' POLITICAL EXILES

June 21, 2018

There are millions of political exiles in the Americas, they are the victims of crimes committed by the dictators from Cuba, Venezuela, Bolivia, Nicaragua, and Correa's Ecuador. People who were forced to abandon their homes by the application of the 21stCentury Socialism's methodology to separate political, social, media leaders, businessmen, professionals, the middle class and the labor force who confront the system, from the national scene. Political exile in the Americas is but another consequence of the crimes committed by the Organized Crime's regimes.

The Latin origin of the word exile "exsilium" derives from the word "exsul interpreted as something removed from its (ex) soil". Exile is the "separation of a person from the land he/she lives on". It is the result of acts and events that compel a person "to alienate himself/herself from the homeland where he/she lives in, or from his/her place of birth". It is the "expatriation" of someone, meaning to leave someone without a homeland, to separate such person from "his/her place of birth or adoptive nation to which a human being is attached by legal, historical, or endearment's links".

There is no voluntary exile because even though the person makes the decision to abandon his/her land, the causes and circumstances that compel the person's departure are forceful, are relentlessly felt, and condition his/her will. The decision to abandon one's homeland is not an act of freedom, quite to the contrary, it is the consequence of violent acts the regime commits or threatens to commit against the victim and under such circumstances of intimidation, the decision to leave is made under duress and cannot be considered as voluntary.

Exile is the consequence and a visible expression of the violation of a person's freedom in order to force such person to live removed from his/her home, family, society, and homeland. It is the forced abdication to remain in a place such person would like to continue living in, in order to protect his personal wellbeing and life. Exile should be a temporary situation that ends with the disappearance of the causes that motivated it as when freedom, democracy, the Rule of Law are recovered, but in many cases, it lasts a lifetime by the prolongation of dictatorial regimes such as Castroist Cuba.

It is precisely Castro's Cuba, the only dictatorship there was in the Americas in 1999, who, with Venezuela's money and oil misappropriated by Hugo Chavez, created the Castroist Chavist system labeled as the Bolivarian project, ALBA, or 21st Century Socialism, against the region's democracies. They expanded the dictatorial mold/model that nowadays controls Cuba, Venezuela, Nicaragua, and Bolivia. A mold/model that Ecuador is trying to exit with Lenin Moreno after Correa's government, and one with which; Mexico, Colombia, El Salvador, Guatemala, Honduras are still threaten by and that Argentina, Peru, Brazil, Panama, Costa Rica, Paraguay (readers can add or edit the list of countries) got rid of.

Until 1999, Cuba's Castroist dictatorship had produced nearly 2 million Cuban exiles, generating a worldwide "diaspora". In almost 20 years under the Castroist Chavist system, it has produced nearly 3 million Venezuelan exiles that have generated another diaspora, with another over 1,500 Bolivian exiles in Brazil, Paraguay, Uruguay, Peru, Spain, and the United States and dozens of Nicaraguan and Ecuadorean exiles.

All the acts and omissions of the Castro's in Cuba, Chavez/ Maduro in Venezuela, Ortega's in Nicaragua, Evo Morales in Bolivia, and Correa in Ecuador to force people into exile, are crimes that reveal they comprise a Transnational Organized Crime network. They respond to a model/mold -as if they were a franchise- created by the Cuban dictatorship and expanded into their territories under the responsibility of the local dictators. A closer look to the objective reality, the international press, and an analysis of cases, corroborate it.

Crimes committed by the Castro's/Diaz Canel, Maduro, Ortega, and Evo Morales, as well as Rafael Correa against people in order to force them into exile, range from; persecution with the aim of physical torture and killing, judicial trials with false accusations heard by "despicable judges", the application of the regime's pseudo-laws violating human rights or of "despicable laws", restricting the freedom of speech or freedom to work, to be employed, or discharge a profession, assassinating the individual's reputation to convert the wrongly accused as an undesirable, subjecting the person into a condition of being defenseless, depriving him/her of a job, food, and much more.

EXTORTION, A TOOL OF ORGANIZED CRIME'S DICTATORSHIPS

June 27, 2018

The regimes from Cuba, Venezuela, Nicaragua, Bolivia and Ecuador under Correa's presidency, replaced politics with criminal practices in order to totally and indefinitely control political power. This reveals an expansion and updating of Cuba's Castroist social control methodology that is seen in concrete facts. Although it is not the only illicit practice, extortion is a key feature of the Castroist Chavist methods in this 21stCentury that is further proof of the Transnational Organized Crime's nature of these dictatorships.

Extortion is "the pressure exerted on someone -through threats- to compel him/her to act in a certain way and obtain a monetary or other type of benefit". The legal definition of extortion includes "the intimidation or serious threat that restricts a person to do, tolerate the doing or not doing of something for the purpose of deriving a benefit or undue advantage for one's self or someone else."

To threaten is "to make it understood through acts or words that harm can befall someone". To intimidate is "to cause or arouse someone to have fear, to inhibit", with the intent that this is to prevent, or repress someone from exercising his personal faculties or rights. It is about instilling fear and the Castroist Chavist methodology does this "legally" through judicial rulings and mandates that range from the content of their "pseudo constitutions", their despicable laws, and the aggregate of directives and institutions they have created and exist with the objective of making extortion the "legal mechanism" of oppression.

The absolute absence of the "Rule of Law", the disappearance of the "separation and independence of the branches of government", are the framework for the use of extortion as a method and means of control. This way, the threat and intimidation in Castro's Cuba, Chavez and Maduro's Venezuela, Ortegas' Nicaragua, Evo Morales' Bolivia, and Correa's Ecuador, functions under the direction of the regime that places its administrative and judicial apparatus with which if the victim does not do or stops doing what the regime wants, imprisonment, prosecution, torture, and the assassination of the victim's reputation follow. All of these done with the regime's control of the press, seizure of assets, misery, ruin, exile or even the victim's death.

Extortion is applied to politicians in order to get their docility or to neutralize them. It is dramatic to see how members of the opposition end up working for the regime and act within the framework or cage of limitations imposed upon them by the dictatorships who alternatively to threatening them can reward them with positions and riches with which it can extort them again afterwards. The Castroist Chavist constitutions have established "the law's retroactivity" and have suppressed or limited parliamentary immunities in order to keep extorting members of the opposition. Hundreds of cases such as; Leopoldo Lopez's in Venezuela and that of his wife Lilian Tintori, trials against former presidents (some already retired) and former Ministers from Bolivia, and members of the opposition in Nicaragua are proof.

Judges, prosecutors, and even attorneys are also extorted. Several cases corroborate this, cases, such as; Venezuela's Judge Maria Lourdes Afiuni's jailing, violations, and tortures; the fired prosecutors and judges who were, afterwards, prosecuted in the case of Magistrate

Gualberto Cusi in Bolivia, as well as the jailing of defense attorneys; the persecution and exile of Magistrates from Venezuela's Supreme Justice Tribunal "the legitimate one in exile", or that of Attorney General Ortega, the assassination of Prosecutor Alberto Nisman in Kirchner's Argentina, and dozens more.

The imprisonment, torture, humiliations, assassinations, and exile started as extortions and are dictatorial warning operations in order to ensure the submission of the system it manipulates "setting precedents" of its decision to use extortion to obtain benefits for the dictator and his Organized Crime's group who is called government, benefits that can range from financial gain, cover up, and impunity, up to the indefinite tenure in government.

No one is free from the government's extortion in Castroist Chavist dictatorships. The judicial system, the police, the Internal Revenue Service's offices, the Labor Department, the Public Administration Service, the Health Department, the Education Department, are all means to extort and subject citizens under the will of the regime. In Cuba, those who "succeed on their own" are closed down and are jailed, in Venezuela and Ecuador important communications' channels were seized and/or forcibly sold to be placed at the service of the regime, in Bolivia journalists are fired under threats from the government, in Nicaragua many assassinations go unpunished. These are countries wherein many citizens can give their testimony of how and how often they were "pressured" with.

DICTATORSHIPS ATTACK WITH MIGRATION, NARCOTICS' TRAFFICKING, AND VIOLENCE

August 28, 2018

Dictatorships from Cuba, Venezuela, Nicaragua, and Bolivia carry out an attack strategy against democracies in the Americas as their best resource to accomplish the objective of indefinitely remaining in power. Cornered by crises, they have gone into an attack mode and the meeting of the Sao Paolo's Forum in Havana was the scenario to launch their new phase of destabilization. The confrontation of the "two Americas", the democratic and the dictatorial, is getting tense because dictatorships attack with forced migration, the generation of internal violence, and destabilization.

In order to remain in power for almost 60 years, Cuba's dictatorship has used this strategy so that their targets be kept busy defending themselves rather than pointing to the Castroist's crimes, or deciding to coexist without wasting time and resources to protect themselves from the threat. Now that the "Castroist Chavist dictatorial empire" is breaking down, the reaction of its Organized Crime's regimes is to attack, given the excellent results this strategy has yielded for the Castro's.

Castroist Chavist dictatorships attack democracies with forced migration due to the humanitarian crisis they have created in Venezuela; with narcotics' trafficking they control and with which they have turned Bolivia and Venezuela into narco-states with cocaine from the FARC and the coca growers' unions of Evo Morales; with the generation of internal violence with infiltrated or the so-called dissidents from the FARC; and with destabilization through the well-greased leadership of social movements and with informants who supplant the press.

Nowadays, Colombia, Brazil, Panama, Ecuador, Guyana, Peru, Chile, Argentina, the United States, in reality all of the region's democratic countries are under the pressure of forced migration caused by Venezuela's dictatorship that has converted one of its shameful problems into a problem for the whole region. Democracies must now deal with problems in; their security, unemployment, provision of health care, their handling of massive numbers of people in transit, the identification, budget, and Human Rights, all because the Castroist Chavist's criminal regime of Nicolas Maduro has transformed its crimes and its effects into a political weapon. Very similar to the so-called "Mariel's exodus" promoted by dictator Fidel Castro against the United States, but many folds greater and for an indefinite period.

All democracies now endure an increase in the "prevalence of drug consumption" produced and/or trafficked by the dictatorships. The President of Argentina has just militarized the border with Bolivia so that its Armed Forces will assist Law Enforcement and Police corps in the fight against cocaine trafficking with which Evo Morales is flooding it. Chile has special control of its border with Bolivia for the same reasons. Brazil already did this, following the impeachment and removal of Rousseff, conducting sustained operations against the drug trafficking that the State of the coca-grower Morales exports. In Paraguay they have just intercepted "a shipment of cocaine hidden in a coal shipment destined for Syria who has relations with Islamic terrorist groups".

THE THREE SOCIAL CLASSES THAT THE CASTROIST CHAVIST SYSTEM IMPOSSES

July 31, 2018

The Marxist statement regarding the struggle between the classes to forge Socialism and advance toward the Communism of a society without social classes, was adopted by Cuba's Castroist regime in the decade of the sixties and replicated by the Castroist Chavist doctrine of the 21stCentury. With that ideological farce, this undertaking has led to the creation of Organized Crime's dictatorships in Cuba, Venezuela, Nicaragua, and Bolivia that have replaced politics with the daily commission of crime and the imposition of three social classes; that of those who have everything because they are part of the group that holds power, that of the majority who live in poverty and are compelled to "try to make it" on a daily basis in order to survive, and that of those who were forced to flee their country.

When the Berlin Wall fell (1989) and the Soviet Union disappeared (1990-1991), Cuba's Castroist dictatorship was left orphaned, devoid of an ideological enunciation, but above it all without the financial aid that allowed it to survive as a parasite, generate guerrillas and generate subversion with which it bloodstained the Americas. Without the Soviet's financial aid, the Castroist system took Cuba to a "Special Period" in which it agonized when in 1999 Hugo Chavez delivered Venezuela's oil resources, and afterwards the entire country to Fidel Castro, thus building the Castroist Chavist doctrine that destroyed Latin America's democracy in the 21stCentury.

The Sao Paolo Forum in 1990 was the dictatorial reaction to the Soviet Communism's catastrophe and was gathered, for the first time, with the objective of addressing the international scenario following the fall of the Berlin Wall and to confront "neo-liberal" policies. It is the tool with which the Castroist dictatorship formulated the "multiplication of the confrontation axis" strategy, going beyond class struggles to the fight against any element that may be useful to destabilize democratic governments.

The 21st Century in the Americas is the history of the Castroist Chavist buildup, apex, and agony, that was presented as a political undertaking and turned out to be criminal. A system that; bloodstained the region again with -as its standard- the violation of Human Rights, destruction of economies, creation of crises, construction of narco-states, institutionalization of corruption ("Lava Jato", as evidence), sustainment of terrorism and threats to peace. Their victims are widespread throughout the world, but the peoples from Cuba, Venezuela, Nicaragua, and Bolivia are their hostages.

The worn-out cliché of "liberation of the peoples" as an "antiimperialist" argument and slogan for massive demonstrations, has remained to become "the peoples' oppression" that is corroborated by the quantity of massacres, assassinations, torture, political prisoners, exiles, and the daily life the people must endure.

Cuba has the highest level of division in their society into three classes: The family/military inner circle that has it all, including great wealth outside of their country and who own the State and manage it as feudal lords through a mixture of managing the needs that they themselves have created and of the institutionalized crime. Cuban people have popularized the verb "to solve" representing they must do whatever it takes in order to survive, and in this realm the regime has achieved equality in misery. Millions of Cubans live in exile and form a sort of diaspora that has lasted decades, over which the regime continues to exert sustained efforts to penetrate and divide.

In Venezuela we can see, in real time, the establishment of a tripartite society. Now the regime has been exposed for multimillion dollar fortunes criminally obtained by members of its elite. Business and restaurants are filled and working well in Caracas for those who have dollars, while the majority of Venezuelans depend on government handouts just to be able to eat. There are no medicines, there are frequent electrical power outages, and the government manages the needs it creates in order to continue generating dependency and political subordination. Venezuelans conjugate the verb "to solve" and the regime boosts the departure of millions of Venezuelans.

Nicaragua under daily massacres by dictator Daniel Ortega, fights valiantly and continues to resist in order not to replicate the agenda lived by Venezuela recently. Bolivia fights to keep dictator Evo Morales from consolidating the electoral farce of again becoming a candidate to place the country in the final phase of constructing societies like that of Cuba and Venezuela.

POLITICIANS MUST DIFFERENTIATE THEMSELVES
FROM ORGANIZED CRIME

September 10, 2018

Seventeen years after the signing of the Interamerican Democratic Charter (IDC), the region suffers four 21st Century Socialism or Castroist Chavist dictatorships, albeit in a fall and in crises but still with enough power to cause much harm with the crimes they commit daily in order to remain in power. These are regimes of Organized Crime that, by their nature, are not in the realm of political activities but that of Organized Crime. This is why it becomes necessary for Americas' leaders and politicians to clearly differentiate themselves from the criminals who hold power in Cuba, Venezuela, Nicaragua, and Bolivia. Not doing so, implies assuming the risk of being accomplices and concealers.

Countries in which the Castroist Chavist, or their allies, have lost power in, such as; Kirchner's Argentina, Lula da Silva and Rousseff's Brazil, Correa's Ecuador, Colombia, and others now suffer corruption's hang-over that has left behind economic crises, political problems, and social confrontation. Moreover, the current democratic governments of those countries are under the pressure of sustained and well financed destabilization efforts, pursued by the authors of serious crimes who still use politics as a means for impunity.

Politics is a public service activity which all citizens have the right to participate in either as electors or elected. For those who choose to aspire and occupy public service functions, concepts of democracy point out that these are positions subject to; the popular mandate born through free and clean elections, the abeyance of the law within a framework of the Rule of Law, are basically temporary and with an obligation to be held accountable.

This is why, among the essential components of democracy, enunciated in Article 3 of the IDC are; the "respect for Human Rights and fundamental freedoms", "access to power and its conduct subject to the Rule of Law", holding "periodic free, fair and just elections based upon the universal and secret suffrage as an expression of the peoples' sovereignty", "the separation and independence of the branches of government".

Because politics is an activity inherent to democracy, the IDC establishes in its Article 4 that "transparency in all governmental activities, probity, the government's responsibility of all public administration, respect for all social rights and freedom of the press, are fundamental components in the exercise of democracy".

By the absence or violation of those fundamental components of democracy, and the components in the exercising of democracy in order to indefinitely perpetuate themselves in power, the regimes from Cuba, Venezuela, Nicaragua, and Bolivia are dictatorships. Their argument to have gotten to power for the first time democratically is useless, because they have counterfeited and supplanted the legal order with a chain of crimes in order to establish a new system of "despicable laws" to allow them to illegitimately and illegally continue to hold power.

The Castro's in Cuba, Maduro in Venezuela, Morales in Bolivia, and Ortega/Murillo in Nicaragua are dictators in the literal sense of the word, because "either by force or violence, they concentrate all power in one person, group, or organization and suppress Human Rights and individual freedoms". Dictatorships, with the aggravating factor that these do not stem from an ideological or political position, but stem from the pure and hard exercise of crime -from corruption, assassinations, torture, counterfeiting, narcotics' trafficking, and terrorism- which configures them as "Organized Crime" organizations, common criminals and not political activities.

Politics is substantially different from what the Castro's/Diaz Canel do, battering and arresting Ladies in White each week, managing their system of slaved-physicians, or distorting a constitutional reform without any freedom in Cuba.

Politics is totally the opposite to crimes of material and ideological falsehood, the use of counterfeited instruments, tortures, persecutions, narcotics' trafficking, and crimes against humanity that are committed by Maduro and his regime in Venezuela, creating a humanitarian crisis that impacts the region and the whole world.

Politics has nothing to do with assassinations, torture, and terror that is conducted without punishment by Ortega/Murillo in Nicaragua.

It's not politics the nth massacre committed by Evo Morales this week against the legal coca-leaf harvesters from the Yungas in Bolivia, or his meeting with the President from Spain's Government in a new act of submissiveness in exchange for the simulation of democracy.

This, and more, is what the peoples from the Americas see and question. This is why politicians and leaders are urged to take concrete actions to differentiate themselves from the criminals of Organized Crime's dictatorships.

CRIMES COMMITTED IN CUBA, VENEZUELA, AND NICARAGUA ARE REPEATED IN BOLIVIA

All criminal schemes to indefinitely hold on to power that were previously used in Cuba, Venezuela, and Nicaragua are now being applied in Bolivia. It is an effort for Evo Morales to be a candidate, because he has ensured his victory in the 2019 elections with yet one other event "to simulate democracy" and through the violation of Human Rights of an entire nation. For Castroist Chavist dictatorships, it is indispensable to keep Bolivia under their control and so they repeat the crimes with which they subjugate Cuba, Venezuela, and Nicaragua.

Evo Morales supplanted the Republic of Bolivia's constitution -it did not allow the continuous reelection of a President- misrepresenting the content of a constitutional reform through Law 2631 of 20 February of 2004 promulgated by Carlos Mesa who without legal competence authorized the convening of a Constituent Assembly when only the partial reform of the constitutions was allowed. With a fraudulent Constituent Assembly in place they brought to the forefront the construction of the Plurinational State that eliminated the Republic of Bolivia with a constitution that is not the one drafted by the Constituent Assembly, because through one other crime yet, the so-called Law 3941 of 21 October of 2008, Morales imposed a different text from the Constituent Assembly's version in an ordinary session of Congress that usurped roles. A series of repeated crimes that created "the lawfulness of the dictatorship".

On 2008, the opposition was the majority in the Senate (Jorge Quiroga led 13 and Doria Medina led 1, a majority of 14 from 27) and could have prevented the elimination of the Republic, however, there was an agreement with Morales, Law 3941 was approved and the Castroist Chavist Constitution was proclaimed as one of national unity, clearing the way for Morales' re-election. The people, along with civic leaders, Governors of six out of nine departments, resisted but Morales overpowered them with several deaths, political prisoners and exiles, with the massacres at Las Americas Hotel, Porvenir in the Northern department of Pando, La Calancha in Sucre, Cochabamba, and more. Another series of repeated crimes that created a "functional (subservient) opposition".

With his Plurinational Constitution of 7 February of 2009, Morales immediately called for elections and re-elected himself for "only one time" on 6 December of 2009. He, however, ran again in the 2014 elections. Formal complaints from the opposition who invoked a document in which Morales committed to be re-elected only one time and guaranteed by Insulza's OAS, were blatantly ignored. The regime's Constitutional Tribunal had issued a ruling authorizing his third consecutive candidacy with the argument that since the Plurinational State had been created in 2009, the 2014 election was Morales' first reelection in the new country.

After taking on his so-called third mandate, Morales called for a referendum election in which YES meant his indefinite perpetuation in power and NO meant that he would not be allowed to be a candidate again. Morales indicated that if the "Yes" would lose, he would go back to his illegal coca leaf harvesting. On 21 February of 2016 the "NO" won, and Bolivia said NO. In-spite of the dictatorial fraud, the Bolivian people's victory at the polls was resounding, but this is when the criminal schemes used in Cuba, Venezuela, and Nicaragua were applied.

Of the thousands of Castroist crimes committed to hold on to power in Cuba, one that stands out is the alleged accident in which they killed Osvaldo Paya, founder and organizer of the "Varela Project" through which and under the protection of the Castroist Constitution, he collected the needed signatures to present to the regime a request for changes. Evo Morales has been accused at The Hague, for the 16 April of 2009 extrajudicial assassinations at the Las Americas Hotel in Santa Cruz and is being held accountable and must respond for dozens of crimes he has committed to take, and hold on to, power.

On 2 December of 2007, Venezuela said NO to Hugo Chavez and his Constitution project and the dictator conceded "defeat only for now", and then manipulating fraudulent electoral processes, subjugated judges, using force, fear, bribery, and Castroist's methodology, he did what he wanted, manipulated a new referendum in 2009 and remained in power until his death.

Nicaragua, with the experience of the Somoza dictatorship, was constitutionally protected, but Daniel Ortega first lowered to 35% the percentage needed to be elected, then controlled the electoral institutions, gained support from opposition members in exchange for their impunity on matters of corruption, and was able to have "his human right to indefinitely run for President" acknowledged through a ruling from a subservient Tribunal, and staged a judicial coup in order to control Congress.

Crimes of the Cuban, Venezuelan, and Nicaraguan dictatorships are being repeated in Bolivia to hold on to power, but will the results be repeated? Bolivian people are mobilizing, they have taken the streets and are ready for a civil resistance campaign and the world cannot ignore it.

SPAINS FOREIGN POLICY TO SUSTAIN DICTATORSHIPS IN LATIN-AMERICA

September 26, 2018

Changes in Spain´s foreign policy regarding freedom, democracy, and the respect for Human Rights in the Americas are for the worse, publicly known and widely noted in just over 100 days that Pedro Sanchez was sworn as the Government´s President. What were inklings suggesting the price for Pablo Iglesias and PODEMOS´ backing to the investiture of the PSOE would be the sustainment of the dictatorships for which Iglesias works and their funding, are now amply evident in Spain´s new foreign policy aiming to sustain the Castroist Chavist dictatorships of Cuba, Venezuela, Nicaragua, and Bolivia.

Article 1.1 of Spain´s constitution establishes that "Spain is constituted as a social and democratic Rule of Law State that promotes; freedom, justice, equality, and political pluralism, as the higher values of its legal framework". In Article 10.2, regarding the rights of the individual, it states "the standards relevant to the basic freedoms and liberties that the Constitution recognizes, shall be interpreted in accordance with the Universal Declaration of Human Rights and the international agreements and treaties on these, ratified by Spain".

A State´s foreign policy is formulated on the basis of principles and self interests and is an expression of its internal policies. Rafael Calduch from Madrid´s Complutense University considers "foreign policy as that part of the general policy formed by the set of decisions and acts through which objectives are defined and the means of a State are utilized in order to generate, modify, or suspend its relations with other actors from the international community"

Within this framework, it is expected for Spain´s foreign policy to be based on the principles of its Constitution and its society, which are; freedom, justice, democracy, and the respect for Human Rights, thus promoting its legitimate interests of; influence, security, economic, commercial, and cultural, expansion and exchanges. It is about the foreign policy of the State and not the party´s or coalition´s in power whose ideology or political position will influence its drafting, but not to the point of violating the fundamental principles of the State.

The objective reality shows that Pedro Sanchez could not have won without the backing of Pablo Iglesias and his PODEMOS political party, reason why he, evidently, entered into a covenant committing a quota or slice of the political pie that deals –among others now being revealed- with the area of communications, information, and international relations in favor of the dictatorial regimes from Cuba, Venezuela, Bolivia, and Nicaragua (besides the FARC´s and others in Colombia) that constituted as the Bolivarian Movement, or 21st Century Socialism promoted and funded PODEMOS in different (some already publicly proven) ways.

In the framework of the OAS´ Interamerican Democratic Charter (IDC), of which Spain is a Permanent Observer, there is no doubt over the dictatorial condition of Cuba, Venezuela, Nicaragua, and Bolivia, because these regimes do not comply with none of the fundamental components of democracy. There is no respect for freedom or basic human rights, there is political judicialized persecution, there are political prisoners and exiles, bloody repression, massacres, and torture. There is no Rule of Law or separation and independence of the branches of government, there is no possibility of free or fair elections, and there is no free political organization or freedom of the press.

While in the Americas there is an on-going fight for freedom and democracy, and the peoples from Cuba, Venezuela, Nicaragua, and Bolivia are the victims of the daily violation of their human rights by the Castroist Chavist regimes who oppress them, the President of Spain's government carries out its new foreign policy of sustainment to the regimes of Diaz-Canel in Cuba, Nicolas Maduro in Venezuela, Evo Morales in Bolivia, and Daniel Ortega in Nicaragua. A quick glance at Pedro Sanchez's and his Ministry of Foreign Affairs' international agenda corroborate this.

Cuban, Venezuelan, Bolivian, and Nicaraguan political exiles and refugees live in Spain, they are the victims of the dictatorships of Castro-Diaz-Canel, Chavez-Maduro, Morales and Ortega. Today, the fight against the dictatorships to restore freedom and democracy is not about a confrontation of the right against the left, it is a matter of fundamental principles against Organized Crime's regimes who have installed narco-states, now supported and backed by Spain's new foreign policy, to the detriment and dishonor of the democratic left who the PSOE always sought to represent.

IS THE USE OF FORCE THE ONLY OPTION DICTATORSHIPS LEAVE

October 9, 2018

Cuba, Venezuela, Nicaragua, and Bolivia are under regimes that after applying all possible simulations and misrepresentation in order to appear to be a revolution, a democracy, populist, leftist, and socialist governments are nothing but Organized Crime's organizations that hold power by force. There have been denouncements, proposals, warnings, and bilateral and multilateral sanctions imposed to help the people to regain freedom and democracy, but these have only been useful to show the stubbornness of dictators who appear to point out that the only other option for them to leave the government is the use of force.

International Law, transformed since the creation of the United Nations Organization (UN), has evolved making every time more relative, or less absolute, the concept of "sovereignty" of the States. Sovereignty, understood as "the supreme power that belongs to an independent State" has progressively yielded competencies to the international arena on the basis of common principles, values, and needs, such as international security and peacekeeping, Human Rights, sanctions against crimes against humanity, the fight against Transnational Organized Crime, democracy, the governments' responsibility to protect, and many other achievements aimed at curbing the practices of those governments who under the allegation of sovereignty oppress, massacre their people and threaten other States.

Besides making the concept of sovereignty as something relative, the UN while establishing the principle of "prohibition to the use of threats or force" acknowledges there are three exceptions that are "the collective actions to keep or reestablish international peace and security through the Security Council, the "legitimate defense" as a natural right, and the "humanitarian intervention".

In this legal context the principle of non-intervention of the Estrada Doctrine of 1930, along with its regional scope, and the self-determination of the nations, are not valid legal arguments because they have been overcome by the creation of new institutions. Besides, alleging self-determination of the nations in order to oppress them and to violate their human rights is but another flaw of the Castroist Chavist dictatorships.

Guidelines are not lacking for the international community, one or several democratic governments, to act against organized crime's dictatorships. There are enough facts and jurisprudence regarding the humanitarian crisis in Venezuela, or the one rapidly turning as the bloodiest crisis in Nicaragua, or the oldest and most lethal in Cuba, or the one most interlinked in Bolivia. Neither is there a lack of causal factors for the people to exercise their supreme right of rebellion against tyranny and oppression as guaranteed in the Universal Declaration of Human Rights.

Dictatorships from Cuba, Venezuela, Nicaragua, and Bolivia are one and the same undertaking, organized as a single subject of international law. Their allegiance with Russia and China to block Security Council resolutions is amply evident with the temporary presidency of Bolivia to manipulate and hinder its agenda. Their allegiance with other dictatorships, such as North Korea is evident. Their ties with regimes who promote Islamic terrorism can no longer be hidden. Support to other governments, such as that of Spain's PSOE, orchestrated by the PODEMOS party, is saddening but nevertheless real.

What started out as the Bolivarian Movement, 21st Century Socialism, and today is simply known as Castroist Chavist dictatorships, is about a group that has left politics behind and has replaced it by the exercise of organized crime that destabilizes democracy and security throughout the Americas. A group that wrongly shelters itself under the guidelines of International Law that it uses as an alibi, but cannot be applied to them because of their criminal nature. They practice open and aggressive meddling in the politics and societies of other States who they threaten, overtly or covertly, and have turned Venezuela, Cuba, Nicaragua, and Bolivia into narco-states and have openly stated at the UN that "the fight against narcotics' trafficking is an instrument of Imperialism to oppress the people" making out of this crime a weapon against the region and the world.

Americas' democracies, nations, peoples, and governments have been placed into a critical situation, one in which the region's dictatorships –as the de-facto regimes they are- have given notice they will not leave the government but by force.

CRIMINAL, ARE THE GOVERNMENTS FROM CUBA, VENEZUELA, BOLIVIA, AND NICARAGUA

November 1, 2018

The defense of freedom and democracy is based on principles, values, and standards that when applied to the objective reality and the scrutiny of facts, bring about conclusions that can be of normalcy, crisis, or the sheer absence of democracy. For a rather extended time, in the Americas we have seen holders of power that besides killing democracy, have installed Transnational Organized Crime's dictatorships. The criminal governments that comprise a consortium are from; Cuba, Venezuela, Bolivia, and Nicaragua.

The parameters to qualify a regime as a dictatorship, an Organized Crime's dictatorship, and a criminal government, are set out by existing universal and regional standards, such as; the United Nations' Charter, the Universal Declaration of Human Rights, The Charter of Bogota, the Covenant of San Jose, the European Union Treaty, the Palermo Convention, the Interamerican Democratic Charter, and many more that are of compulsory adherence by the States, governments, and the citizenry.

In this context, in my column "To Differentiate and Separate Politics from Organized Crime" published this past 11th of March, I stated -and today reiterate- that: "Americas' reality is worsening because the Castroist Chavist system shows that its actions and objectives are not of a political nature but totally belong to the Organized Crime arena. Separating those countries with democracy from those with dictatorships is no longer enough. The regimes from Cuba, Venezuela, Bolivia, Nicaragua, and Correa's Ecuador, besides having installed de-facto governments harnessing and concentrating all power and being sustained by violence, belong in the Transnational Organized Crime arena".

The order of the countries under criminal control; Cuba, Venezuela, Bolivia, and Nicaragua, corresponds to the historical time in which each of them began their criminal regime. Cuba, since 1959, will soon celebrate 60 years with the Castro's, Venezuela established the Organized Crime's regime with Hugo Chavez in 1999, Bolivia did it in 2006 with Evo Morales, and in 2007 Daniel Ortega began the control of Nicaragua.

Proof that these are dictatorships is their constant violation of all essential components of democracy. These regimes have people politically persecuted, imprisoned, and exiled, are guilty of massacres and torture as acts of the government, they do not have either freedom of the press or Rule of Law, there is no separation and independence of the branches of government, and have turned the Judicial Branch into a mechanism for political repression, they have turned elections into a permanent fraud in order to supplant the will and the sovereignty of the people so they can indefinitely remain in power.

The international press, with respect to Cuba, Venezuela, Bolivia, and Nicaragua, provides some of the common features of those in power who, under the helm of Cuba, are associated in operations that range from; squelching street demonstrations, are aimed at destabilizing unity in protests, are used for propaganda and for caravans, up to violent eruptions in international forums such as at the UN where "diplomats" from Cuba and Bolivia attacked the speech of OAS' Secretary Almagro on the issue of political prisoners in Cuba.

Further proof that these are part of Transnational Organized Crime are the political prisoners there are in Cuba, Venezuela, Bolivia, and Nicaragua, all imprisoned with the same methodology directed by the Castroist system. Cuba has over 120, Venezuela has nearly 500, Bolivia over 80, and Nicaragua over 300. One other proof yet are the numbers of Cuban and Venezuelan exiles that can add up to millions, the Bolivian exiles that, according to data from ACNUR, are in excess of 1,200 and the Nicaraguan exiles who increase in numbers each day.

More corroborating proof are the narcotics' trafficking activities that have caused Venezuela and Bolivia to be identified as narco-states, the first as the center point of commercializing the FARC's and Evo Morales' coca growers' cocaine from Bolivia that have flooded the region and the world with an increase by 20 times of the amount of illegal coca harvested, the expulsion of the DEA and the "international political revindication" of narcotics' trafficking such as what Morales did at the UN in 2016 stating that "the fight against narcotics' trafficking is an instrument of North American Imperialism to oppress the nations."

Whoever doesn't see this entire scenario and excludes any of the "four criminal governments" from an analysis or has a different conclusion, is wrong or are victims of the permanent penetration and cover up efforts the dictatorships conduct throughout the democratic world, and owes an explanation.

ESSAY ON THE FUNCTIONAL POLITICAL OPPOSITION IN A DICTATORSHIP

November 28, 2018

By its nature and objectives political opposition is an inseparable part of democracy, reason why when it is deprived of the fundamental components of democracy it is rendered unrealizable. When democracy is supplanted, political opposition disappears, resistance is birthed and everything that is attributed to the opposition is but a simulation in order to legitimize the regime. This is known as "the functional opposition in a dictatorship" that far from being a true opposition is complicity.

Political opposition is the "expression of contradiction, indispensable in a democratic process of molding the political will and is the portrayal of freedom, human rights, pluralism, and the alternance in government" and must have, as an indispensable feature "the possibility to get to be the government through elections". Resistance is "a set of people who, through different means, oppose invaders or a dictatorship."

Democracy is "the form of government in which political power is yielded by the citizenry", it is "the political doctrine according to which sovereignty rests in the people who yield power either directly or through their representatives". Dictatorship is the "political regime that, through force or violence, converges all power into one person, group, or organization, and represses human rights and individual freedoms."

For all of Americas' governments, democracy is a human right "fundamental for the nations' social, political, and economic development". The Interamerican Democratic Charter sets out -amongst others- as fundamental components of democracy; "the respect for Human Rights and basic individual freedoms, access to political power and its conduct subject to the Rule of Law, holding of periodic elections that are free, fair, secret, and are based on universal suffrage concepts, as an expression of the people's sovereignty, the existence of a plurality of political parties and organizations, and the separation and independence of the branches of government".

If only just one of the fundamental components of democracy is lacking, there is no democracy, because fundamental is "that which constitutes the nature of things, the permanent, the most important and characteristic of a thing." There is no half-hearted democracy, and labels such as; hybrid or imperfect, are interested fallacies that may be plausible but are of invalid political and academic reasoning in order to continue disguising dictatorial regimes as democracies.

In this legal and conceptual context, it is easily verifiable that the regimes from Cuba, Venezuela, Nicaragua, and Bolivia, are dictatorships since long ago. Cuba with the Castro brothers since 1959, Venezuela with Chavez since 2007 or before, and today without a doubt with Maduro, Nicaragua since -at least- 2009 with Ortega, and Bolivia since 2006 with Morales. These are regimes that do not abide by any of the fundamental components of democracy, perfectly fit into the mold and concept of a dictatorship, and in which there is no possibility to ever be a true political opposition.

Public and notorious events show the regimes from Cuba, Venezuela, Nicaragua, and Bolivia to; violate Human Rights and individual basic freedoms as their governmental policy; have politically persecuted, imprisoned, or exiled; commit political crimes, crimes against humanity, and Transnational Organized crimes, all with impunity. The Rule of Law is absent because the dictator is the law; there is no chance of free or fair elections; the Judicial Branch is an instrument for political repression and persecution; there is no freedom of the press; there is no separation and independence of the branches of government, and more.

In that type of situation there are those who claim to be, and act as, "political opposition" and that beyond the inadequate use of such title they pretend to make Venezuelans, Nicaraguans, Bolivians, and other throughout the world, believe they really oppose the regime. People ask, however, if; do they really believe there is democracy? Are they free to do as they please? Is there really pluralism? Does the system respect their human rights and individual basic freedoms? Do they have a chance to climb to power through elections?... and the answer to all of those questions is a resounding NO.

What the objective reality reveals is that Castroist Chavist, or 21st Century Socialism dictatorships, in the pursuit of their own interests, keep and sustain a functional political opposition that legitimizes the regime. This opposition is functional because its existence is allowed, encouraged, and sustained considering the easiness, usefulness, and convenience of their use for the continuity of the regime.

We must restore those in-good-faith opponents, because they exist and remain in the fight comprising the resistance. It is indispensable, however, to also identify those who became functional opponents solely by need, in order to survive, or were pressured, coerced, or intimidated, from those opponents who became the functional opposition driven by financial and personal interests, interests to preserve their estate, or to improve their position and increase their estate either directly or through concessions, permits, contracts, and any other type of dealings with the government and in a system plagued with corruption.

We can no longer continue in the deception that there are real opponents in Transnational Organized Crime's dictatorships whose cruelty and corruption have been proved and are beyond any doubt. Functional opponents sustain dictatorships because they know they will fall when the regimes fall and this is the biggest part of the problem why the regaining of democracy is taking so long.

ABSTAINING IN ORDER TO CONFRONT THE DICTATORSHIP'S ELECTORAL SIMULATION

December 6, 2018

Dictatorships of the 21st Century in the Americas are the result of the expansion of Cuba's dictatorship today comprised by Venezuela, Nicaragua, and Bolivia. Having originally climbed to power through elections, they successively staged several coups in order to supplant the existing constitutional order until they created a legal bureaucratic scheme contrary to democracy. With their methodology that includes fraud and other crimes, they manipulate the electoral system to indefinitely retain power. They have turned elections into a derisive simulation, something that must be dealt with one of the options of civil resistance, abstention from voting, in order to recover democracy.

Holding "periodic, free, fair, elections and based on universal and secret suffrage as an expression of the peoples' sovereignty" is an essential component of democracy made mandatory by Article 3 of the Interamerican Democratic Charter, that is possible if only concurs with "respect for human rights and basic individual freedoms" the "Rule of Law", a "plural regime of political parties and organizations", and the "separation and independence of the branches of government".

The dictatorial nature of a regime is proven by its violation of all essential components of democracy through the supplanting of the democratic order, manipulation of constituent assemblies, referendums, consults and elections, down to the imposition of a fraudulent legal framework, a "legal" scheme, that nowadays is the legal system in existence in Venezuela, Nicaragua, Bolivia, and Correa's Ecuador. It's all about the dictatorial statutes that have replaced the institutionalism of the "Republic" with "despicable laws" to ensure their impunity and indefinite tenure in the government.

Hugo Chavez and Nicolas Maduro in Venezuela, Daniel Ortega in Nicaragua, Evo Morales in Bolivia, and Rafael Correa in Ecuador, eliminated the separation and independence of the branches of government using the mechanism of electoral manipulation. They elevated the electoral institution as "another branch of the government" and by designating their officials they made disappear any possibility of impartiality, manipulating every area; from the identification processing of the citizenry, their voter's registration, their electoral districts, rendering the eligibility of candidates, their campaigns, and the results.

The repeated, flawed, electoral processes with manipulated outcomes were useful to the Castroist Chavist dictators to insist in presenting themselves as "Presidents" and to make their inadmissible dictatorships into a mockery of democracy. When they lost elections or referendums, in-spite of fraud and manipulation, they used further manipulation of the other branches of the government they also controlled, such as the Judicial and/or Legislative in order to illegally and illegitimately remain in power, just as it happened with Chavez in 2005-2007, with Maduro in 2015 and 2018, with Ortega since 2009, with Morales in 2009, 2014, and current crimes being perpetrated in preparation for 2019.

When an electoral process lacks the conditions of democracy and there is no guarantee of transparency, this cannot be free and fair elections and then the opposition and the resistance have but only two options; participate or abstain. The opposition's participation in elections under a Castroist Chavist dictatorship uniformly presents candidates who are "functional" meaning useful, for the regime, and are rife of fraud, manipulation of results, and guarantee the permanence in power of the dictator.

Venezuela has taught us at least three ways to deal with elections under a dictatorship: 1. The total abstention in the Parliamentary Elections of 2005 that enabled for Chavez's total control at a moment in time of dictatorial consolidation. 2. The opposition's unity with the Mesa de la Unidad Democratica (MUD in Spanish) political party that won the presidential election of 2013 that it was not able to defend, and that had also won the Parliamentary Elections of 2015 with the control of 2/3 of the ignored, then persecuted, and then supplanted National Assembly by Maduro. 3. The abstention at the 2018 presidential elections that took Nicolas Maduro's dictatorship to the illegality and illegitimacy, with the concurrence of two opposition's candidates who were visibly very functional and an estimated abstention rate of 70%.

When the regime's candidate controls all; the policy, the electoral and judicial officials, when he/she has all of the country's and corruption's resources, he/she can exert intimidation and grant favors to electors and elected, can control the press, and can have a monopoly of the electoral propaganda and there is no chance or possibility to have free elections.The Venezuelan people's abstention in May of 2018 is an option that delegitimizes the regime and marks its unavoidable fall. Abstaining from voting is civil resistance to dictatorships that make out of manipulated elections their alibi to simulate a non-existent democracy.

TO RUN AS A CANDIDATE IN A DICTATORSHIP IS TO DRESS UP A TYRANT AS A DEMOCRAT

December 18, 2018

The Castroist Chavist regimes in Venezuela, Nicaragua, and Bolivia are electorally-fed dictatorships who have, as their main objective, the holding of manipulated elections through which they seek to simulate the existence of democracy. These are façades with neither freedom nor justice, in which there is no chance for a member from the opposition to ascend into power, even if the elections are won. Under these conditions, those who present themselves as candidates become functional accomplices to the regime's needs that, with their participation, dress up the tyrants as democrats.

I conceptualize the "electoral-fed dictatorship" as "the political regime that by force or violence garners and concentrates all political power in one person or one group, represses human rights and fundamental individual rights, and uses elections as the means for the simulation and propaganda in order to indefinitely remain in power".

The essence of an election is "to choose or prefer" someone for a determined objective. Politically speaking, it is "a decision-making process in which the citizenry elects with its vote a person for a specified government position". Elections are part of the electoral process that is "the set of events conducted in phases, according to the Constitution and laws that govern electoral authorities, political parties, and the citizenry in order to periodically renew the Government's elective members".

In the Americas, elections solely by themselves are not democracy. They are an essential component of democracy instituted by the Inter American Democratic Charter as "the celebration of elections that are periodic, free, fair, and based on universal and secret suffrage rules and as an expression of the peoples' sovereignty." They must be comprised by, and have the integration of, "the respect for Human Rights and fundamental individual freedoms", the existence of "the Rule of Law" and the existence of a "regime of several political parties and organizations" and have the "separation and independence of the branches of government".

For elections to be free and fair, there must be "conditions of democracy" in existence, this is the minimum presence of the essential components of democracy that will enable all citizens to be either voters or be elected, will guarantee an equity of options to the candidates, transparency in the process, impartiality in the electoral authorities, offer guarantees of resources with impartial judges, with freedom of association, freedom of expression, freedom of the press, and guarantees against electoral fraud, timeliness, and more.

Without conditions of democracy, elections are turned into a mockery of the popular (peoples') will, transformed into an illegal and criminal instrument for the perpetuation of someone in power, a system plagued with fraud, corruption, and of NOT being an election, a system such as the one imposed in Cuba, Venezuela, Nicaragua, and Bolivia that is an "electorally-fed dictatorship", wherein dictators have transformed elections into a saddening chain of governmental crimes that are committed with impunity and recurrence.

Elections where human rights and basic individual freedoms are violated, with politically persecuted, imprisoned, or exiled, where there is no freedom of the press, where voters' registration and information are manipulated, wherein there is no "Rule of Law" and the "separation and independence of the branches of government" is inexistent because all power is garnered by and concentrated in the head of a group who at the same time is also a candidate to be perpetuated in power. These are not elections, it is fraud, it is organized crime in action.

In the 21st Century, the longest, most enriching -yet terrible-experience as to what to do from the opposition's and democratic resistance perspective in an electorally-fed dictatorship is that of Venezuela, that during almost twenty years has tried practically everything and has included the "double abstention" that consists of not having candidates and not voting or voting in blank. This extreme recourse of civil resistance to confront the dictatorship has proven to be very effective "to illegitimate" the regime, to once and for all remove its democratic façade, put an end to its simulation of democracy, and reveal the crimes committed by the holders of power.

Whoever presents himself/herself as a candidate from the opposition in an "electoral-fed" dictatorship has no justification because his/her presence serves but one sole purpose, that "to legitimize" the "candidate dictator". Moreover, when there are several and even many candidates -which facilitates the candidate dictator's manipulation- as is now happening in Bolivia, to so-called candidates from the opposition are mere accomplices in the shameful role of dressing up the tyrant as a democrat.

AS LONG AS CUBA IS A DICTATORSHIP, THE AMERICAS WILL BE ENDANGERED

December 28, 2018

After 60 years of dictatorship in Cuba, the criminal aftermath the Castroist regime causes is extreme and remains unpunished. The massacre and subjugation of its people, executions by firing squads, imprisonments, millions of exiles, destabilization, invasions, urban and rural guerrillas, terrorism, narcotics' trafficking, assassinations, torture, human trafficking, discrediting and assassination of reputations, conspiracies, operations against international peace and security. There isn't one crime, whether it be a common crime, political crime, or a crime against humanity, that Fidel Castro and members of his regime have not committed and continue to commit. As long as Cuba remains a dictatorship, the people, the nations, the governments, and the countries of the Americas will be endangered.

Cuba's dictatorship is the de-facto regime that took over Havana on the 1st of January of 1959, it is sustained by force and violence and had concentrated all power in Fidel Castro who governed until 31 July of 2006 when, due to illness, deteriorating health, and old age, transferred all power to his brother Raul Castro. On the 18th of April of 2018, the regime started a new dictatorial transition scheme by designating as "President" an individual named Miguel Diaz-Canel, thus placing underway a reform to its dictatorial constitution. Cuba's dictatorship today controls the dictatorships in Venezuela, Nicaragua, and Bolivia.

As an acknowledgement of its dangerousness, on the 31st of January of 1962 Cuba was expelled from the Organization of American States (OAS) because its membership was "incompatible" with the Inter-American system. On 3 June of 2009 at the initiative of Venezuela, Ecuador, Bolivia, Nicaragua, and Honduras, the OAS retracted on Cuba's expulsion and invited it back, but Cuba has not returned.

In 1961, Cuba's dictatorship birthed; Nicaragua's National Liberation Army (ELN)* afterwards converted into the Sandinista National Liberation Front (FSLN), then later converted into 13th of November Revolutionary Movement (MR13N), and the Revolutionary Armed Forces (FAR) in Guatemala. In 1962, it birthed Venezuela's National Liberation Armed Forces (FALN), the Colombian Self Defense Forces turned into the Southern Block Forces afterwards turned into the Colombian Revolutionary Armed Forces (FARC). In Peru, it birthed the National Liberation Army (ELN) and the Leftist Revolutionary Movement (MIR), in Bolivia the National Liberation Army (ELN), in Uruguay the Tupamarus, as an urban guerrilla, in Argentina the Montoneros, and in the 70's the People's Revolutionary Army (ERP), in Brazil the Revolutionary Movement 8 (MR8), and many more. Practically, the Castroist movement did not spare any one single country from staining it with blood with the guerrillas.

The "missile crisis" that started on 15 October of 1962 by the U.S. discovery of Soviet bases for the launching of Soviet intermediate range nuclear missiles from Cuba's territory, revealed how far the Cuban dictatorship was willing to go to take the world to a nuclear war that was avoided through an agreement -unknown to Fidel Castro- between the Soviet Premier Nikita Khrushchev and President John F. Kennedy. History shows that the dictator Castro and his regime promoted this nuclear aggression. Che Guevara wrote about this to be "a chilling example of a nation that is willing to atomically sacrifice itself so that its ashes may be the foundation of new societies".

In the decades of the 70's and 80's they converted the guerrillas into terrorism involved in narcotics' trafficking, kidnapping, and extortion, with Colombia's FARC as the most noteworthy case. Castro's involvement with narcotics' trafficking is well documented, including his relationship with Pablo Escobar. Facing the disappearance of the Soviet Union and the fall of the Berlin wall, they organized the Forum of Sao Paolo and Hugo Chavez saved them from further going under in "the special period" in 1999 birthing what we now know as the "Castroist Chavist" doctrine with which they recurrently commit and multiply their crimes in Venezuela, Nicaragua, and Bolivia, and threaten the entire region.

Recently, on the 7th of December of 2018, the OAS held a Conference on Human Rights in Cuba, in which Secretary General Almagro rightfully declared that "as long as Cuba is a dictatorship, persecuting, torturing, and silencing its people and teaching others to persecute, to assassinate, to torture and to silence, we cannot have a hemisphere lacking of bad habits that affect freedom, democracy and peace". Leaders from the Americas know this to be true, but many of them keep silence.

Cuba's dictatorship is the greatest threat to the Americas, starting with the United States, its main enemy. Today, the Cuban regime jostles others with the presence of Russia, China and Iran in the region, with Islamic terrorism, with narcotics' trafficking, with the migratory pressure, the destabilization of governments, the violation of human rights, with political prisoners, torture, exile, and all types of crime. They never stopped committing crimes and today they do so openly, directly and through its operators, the other dictators; Nicolas Maduro, Daniel Ortega, and Evo Morales.

MADURO'S AND MORALES' ORGANIZED CRIMINAL GROUP DEFENDS ORTEGA

January 4, 2018

The use of the Interamerican Democratic Charter (IDC) against Daniel Ortega's and Rosario Murillo's regime has sparked Nicolas Maduro's and Evo Morales' violent defense. When we consider the objective reality of assassinations, torture, political imprisonments, violation of human rights, and all types of crime being committed, Maduro's and Morales' reaction, on behalf of Venezuela and Bolivia and in favor of the Nicaraguan regime, is a public confession and explicit evidence of the existence of an "organized criminal group" under the direction of Cuba of which they are part of.

The current international system has standards and procedural guidelines to stop and punish crimes committed by those illegal holders of power. Besides using the IDC, the United Nations' organization is an opened option, but in the case of Nicaragua, Cuba, Venezuela, and Bolivia, the use of the Palermo Convention on Transnational Organized Crime would be faster and more effective.

Article 2 of the Palermo Convention indicates that "by organized criminal group, it shall be understood to be a structured group of three or more persons that exists during a certain time and deliberately acts for the purpose of committing one or more serious crimes, or those crimes listed under this present convention, with the intent to gain, directly or indirectly, a financial or other benefit or material gain". It further defines that "by serious crime, it shall be understood that behavior that constitutes a punishable crime, punished with incarceration for a maximum of at least four years or with a greater sentence".

I repeat, the dictators from Cuba, Venezuela, Nicaragua, and Bolivia do not belong in the political realm and function within the realm of Transnational Organized Crime in order to indefinitely hang-on to power. Sixty years of dictatorship in Cuba are a vivid example of an endless, repetitive, series of crimes "iter criminis" that commits every and all types of recurring crime with impunity, and under the protection of political power. At the end of 2018, the axis of confrontation in the Americas is not ideological but factual and is "Transnational Organized Crime against Democracy."

In Nicaragua, massive street protests began on 18 April of 2018 and Daniel Ortega and Rosario Murillo placed underway the application of measures and methods for social-control, designed, tested and tried by Cuba's Castroist dictatorship. Up to now, this methodology has -in a sustained and recurrent manner- caused almost 500 deaths with evident assassinations, over 2,500 injured, more than 2,000 political prisoners subjected to torture, and an undetermined number of exiled, violating individual human rights and basic freedoms.

Ortega's and Murillo's crimes have been, and are, committed from their role as Nicaragua's Heads of State, using the total concentration of political, legislative, judicial, economic, military, and police power and by the use of massive propaganda, using the Castroist Chavist, or 21st Century Socialism's system, to ascend to power through elections and then dismantle democratic institutions afterwards, replacing them through the application of despicable laws, eliminating the Rule of Law, the separation and independence of the Branches of Government, annulling the opposition and supplanting it with functional accomplices.

Both; the Castroist Chavist system of building "21st Century Socialism dictatorships", as well as the methodology for social control based on fear and the violation of human rights, are the creation of Cuba's Castroist dictatorship. These have been applied for the past 20 years, starting by Venezuela with Hugo Chavez then Nicolas Maduro, in Ecuador with Rafael Correa, in Bolivia with Evo Morales, and in Nicaragua with Daniel Ortega. Other States, such as Argentina with the Kirchner's, Brazil with Lula and Rousseff, and several Central America's countries as El Salvador and Honduras, were well advanced undertakings, but were contained by democracy.

When dictator Nicolas Maduro babbles "the reprehensible Luis Almagro, shows once-again, his servility to the interests of the United States' foreign policy ..." and dictator Evo Morales fumes "we reject that by the Empire's instructions and with the intent to topple governments, the OAS pretends to apply the Democratic Charter to Nicaragua" we are witnessing a response -orchestrated from Cuba- of the Transnational Criminal Group that without any reservation justifies the crimes that are committed in Nicaragua, because -following this very same agenda- they commit the same crimes in Venezuela where the IDC has already been applied, and in Bolivia where sooner than later the IDC will be applied.

3

CUBA

TRANSFER OF POWER IN CUBA, ANOTHER DOING OF ORGANIZED CRIME

April 25, 2018

Falsehood, deception and impunity are some of the key features of the transfer of power that has just taken place in Cuba. It is not a political event but another cog of the chain of crime to continue controlling Cuba as a State, subjecting its people and directing from therein, the most important network of Transnational Organized Crime that utilizes politics as a cover. Every step of the so called "transfer of power in Cuba" is further proof of the "serious crimes" that are committed by the "structured group" of organized crime holding political power there.

Falsehood is that which lacks truth, it is "a crime consisting of the alteration or simulation of the truth with relevant consequences, made in public documentation…". To deceive is "to make someone believe that something that is false is truthful" it is "to create an illusion" in other words to produce an image that lacks real truth. Whenever those who commit crimes of deception, and simulations violating human rights and subject their nation's people to commit further crime in the international environment, and still remain unpunished we are facing impunity.

Falsehood as an essential element of the Castroist regime in Cuba is proven by the so called "elections" for popular power, held in Cuba, on the 11th of March of 2018 which were presented as "parliamentary elections" with 8.7 million voters registered of which 7.4 million voted and by an astounding 94.42% of the ballots "elected" 605 representatives who, in-turn "elected" members of the State's Council, the President, and Vice-President by an average of 99.83% of the votes.

It is blatant proof of the crimes of; falsehood, deliberate misrepresentation, and supplanting, because for there to be "elections" there must be "freedom to choose" and to "choose is to select or prefer someone" something that does not exist in a political system with a single party, with candidates who are subservient to the government, with on-going repression, political prisoners, without true political opposition, in a system of totalitarian control. There are no real elections in Cuba. What the regime orchestrates as elections is simply the sequel of its crimes, attempting to make everyone believe that in Cuba voters may "elect" when, in reality, as an oppressed nation –not a civic nation- under pressure and duress, is compelled to abide by the orders and mandates of those illegitimate holders of power.

All of this deliberate misrepresentation is done in order to commit another fraud consisting of "installing" under the title of "President" someone who is willing and able to partially fulfill those functions which due to questions of age and health the chieftain of the organization Raul Castro –who also forcibly inherited his position due to the illness and death of Fidel Castro- is no longer able to perform

Can there be a President in a State in which there are no "free and fair elections based on universal and secret suffrage as an expression of the people's sovereignty?" Of course NOT. It is but another noteworthy effort of deception, attempting to present a "dictator" as "President", and in the particular case of Miguel Diaz Canel's selection, it would seem an effort of selecting a deteriorated dictator.

The soap box opera played out in Cuba could be a successful comedy if it would not have the gravest consequence of oppressing nearly 11.5 million Cubans, of manipulating the ballot box and sustaining through criminal practices the regimes of Venezuela, Bolivia, and Nicaragua (now identified as narco-States), of threatening the region with crime, terrorism, destabilization, and the sequestering of democratic governments. In the midst of a communications' revolution, the Castroist system pretends to present this as a transition and election of a new President. A simple operation of tweaking its inner circle, in order to continue committing crime under the guise of politics and Government who they control.

Both; existing literature, along with information from open public sources, indicate that in the mafia when the Capo or Mafioso chieftain gets old, there is a meeting of the families who through their representatives "elect" the successor who the Capo had previously identified. The elder Capo, Mafioso Chieftain, retains power and the successor Capo operates under his instructions and protection. The function of the elder Capo is to wield real power because he controls the heads of the mafia's familial clans and the objective of the election of a successor is to enable for a smooth generational transition to take place among the Mafiosi, but neither a change in the system, nor a change in the purpose of the criminal undertakings they handle. Is there a difference of how the mafia handles this and what we are now seeing in Cuba?

The world's democracies know this. The hope now is for them to realize the danger that represents any transfer of power as the doing of Organized Crime.

FOUR ARE THE DICTATORSHIPS; CUBA, VENEZUELA, NICARAGUA, AND BOLIVIA

June 14, 2018

The Organization of American States' (OAS) 48[th]Period of Ordinary Sessions has fulfilled the organization's objective of "promoting and consolidating democracy" declaring Venezuela's electoral process and regime as illegitimate. It is a historical event that consolidates the OAS' recovery, following a shameful period in which it was under the control of, and was an instrument for, "the 21[st]Century Socialism" today known as "Organized Crime's Dictatorships". This is a reminder that there are still "two Americas", the one democratic and the other dictatorial comprised by four dictatorships; Cuba, Venezuela, Nicaragua, and Bolivia.

In the Americas, democracy is obligatory for those governments that are part of the OAS. It is neither an abstract concept relegated to theorist considerations, nor is it a debatable question because it is contained in a mandatory text that is the Interamerican Democratic Charter (IDC) subscribed in Lima on the 11[th]of September of 2001. The term "Charter" in International Law "is used to designate official instruments of grave solemnity and significance, such as the organizational charter of an international organization". The OAS has two charters; the Charter of Bogota which birthed the organization and the Interamerican Democratic Charter, with which democracy was institutionalized. That is the importance and indispensability of a mandatory standard that dictatorships pretend to dismiss as a simple proclamation.

Article 1 of the IDC mandates that *"America's people have the right to democracy and their governments have the obligation to promote and defend it"*. Article 3 declares that "representative democracy's essential components are, among others; respect for human rights and basic freedoms, access to power and its discharge subject to the Rule of Law, the conduct of periodic, free, fair elections based on the universal and secret suffrage as an expression of the people's sovereignty, the plurality of political parties and organizations, and the separation and independence of the branches of government".

A dictatorship is "the political regime that, through force or violence, concentrates all power in one person or in one group or organization and represses human rights and individual basic freedoms". Applying the concept of the IDC, there is a dictatorship when "a kind of government that concentrates power in one individual or an elite, violating any of the essential components of democracy" is established. These are the features that we now see in Cuba, Venezuela, Nicaragua, and Bolivia that are dictatorships.

Democracy is finally reacting, following almost two decades of imposition by the Cuban dictatorial mold with Venezuela's oil resources from the Castro-Chavez alliance, followed by the Castroist's control of Nicolas Maduro's regime. This made the OAS, with Insulza as its General Secretary, an instrument for the expansion and cover up of dictatorships that were strengthened by an unraveled Transnational Organized Crime's scheme known as "Lava Jato" with "the Forum of Sao Paolo" that involved bribes and payoffs for the contracting of mega construction projects with the participation of Lula da Silva from Brazil and that are still covered up in Cuba, Venezuela, Nicaragua, and Bolivia.

The OAS' current General Secretary, Luis Almagro, broke the scheme in the case of Venezuela, applying the IDC with his reports and his sustained fight that created the "Almagro Doctrine". The new U.S. foreign policy set by President Trump in June of 2017 has began to be applied -almost a year thereafter- with efforts by Secretary of State Mike Pompeo and signals the return to the principles that coincide with his national security's interests. The Group from Lima, Mexico's leadership, the courage of Costa Rica and Chile, Argentina and Brazil's decision, the change in Colombia, have released 19 important votes, but are not enough.

Among the 11 countries that abstained, Ecuador stands out with indications of its departure from the group of dictatorships that was formerly tied to by Correa. Nicaragua, one of the dictatorships that abstained, surely did so in exchange for the lenient treatment it received, and there are still those countries that are still dependent on the dictatorial oil or fear. Those supporting the Venezuelan dictatorship are; Cuba who showed that it controls -from the outside- the island nations of Dominica and Saint Vincent, LG, and Evo Morales' Bolivia whose illegitimate tenure in power depends of Venezuela and Cuba's dictatorships.

We cannot afford to forget there are four dictatorships; Cuba, Venezuela, Nicaragua, and Bolivia who comprise a Transnational Organized Crime's group.

APPLY THE PALERMO CONVENTION FOR THE HUMAN TRAFFICKING OF CUBAN PHYSICIANS

November 21, 2018

Under the spurious appearance of being "cooperators or internationalists", Cuba's dictatorship runs a system involved in lending physicians and other personnel in "conditions of slavery" to Latin American governments and others. In Brazil, this program known as "Mais Medicos" (More Physicians in Portuguese) was abruptly ended by the Castroist regime's decision in order to deny Brazil's President-Elect Jair Bolsonaro's request for the Cuban physicians to; receive the totality of their salaries, have the right to have their credentials ratified, and not be forced to be separated from their families. Details, threats, and the coercion with which the regime is forcing the return of these physicians to Cuba, make the United Nations' protocol on Transnational Organized Crime's "Human Trafficking" applicable.

The "Protocol to prevent, repress, and punish Trafficking in Persons, especially women and children" is in Annex II of the Convention that in its Article 3.a states: "Trafficking in persons" shall mean the recruitment, transportation, transfer, harboring or receipt of persons, by means of the threat or use of force or other forms of coercion, of abduction, of fraud, of deception, of the abuse of power or of a position of vulnerability or of the giving or receiving of payments or benefits to achieve the consent of a person having control over another person, for the purpose of exploitation. Exploitation shall include, at a minimum, the exploitation of the prostitution of others or other forms of sexual exploitation, forced labor or services, slavery or practices similar to slavery, servitude or the removal of organs."

The Protocol in Annex II, further states that: "The consent of a victim of trafficking in persons…shall be irrelevant…" This Convention was signed in Palermo in December of 2000. Brazil ratified the Palermo Convention and its annexes on 29 January of 2004, Cuba ratified the Palermo Convention on 9 February of 2007 and accepted the Protocol on Trafficking in Persons on 20 June of 2013.

The Mais Medicos program was started by President Rousseff on the 8th of July of 2013, and from the start was accused of being a system of slavery because 70% of the salary Brazil paid for every physician went to benefit the Cuban regime, the Pan American Health Organization (OPS in Spanish) who played the role of intermediary retained a portion of the salary, and the physician received what was left. The so-called internationalists are forced to leave their families behind in Cuba as hostages to secure the physicians' subjugation and return

Under this charade, Cuban physicians and other personnel serve in Venezuela, Bolivia, Ecuador since Correa's presidency, and other countries. In Venezuela this program was labeled "Deep in the Barrio Mission" and consists of over 31,000 Cubans with the same complaint of the Castroist regime's misappropriation of their salaries. In Bolivia this Cuban program known as "Operation Miracle" has led Bolivian physicians to conduct massive street protests against the presence of thousands of Cuban physicians who they accuse of medical mal-praxis and involvement in the internal politics to favor Evo Morales' regime. In Ecuador, the Castroist regime has forced the "cooperators" to use "twitter, with a mandatory quota" to spread messages in defense of the enslaving program.

The newspaper New Herald back in 2014 had already reported that "nearly 3,000 Cuban professionals, most of whom were Physicians had deserted from the program in Venezuela in 2013". This week, journalist Andres Oppenheimer refers to this issue as "the scandalous slavery of Cuban physicians in Brazil" reiterating that the physicians' families "remain in Cuba as hostages to reduce the risk of massive desertions" accusing the OPS/OMS for their participation. Journalist Mario J. Penton posted on twitter a video showing a Cuban official coercing "anyone who dares to ask for asylum in Brazil will not be able to comeback to Cuba for eight years."

Ample proof shows that members of Cuba's dictatorship led by Raul Castro, high level executives from the OPS and officials from the Brazilian government with Rousseff and the Workers' Party, formed a "group of Organized Crime" to commit "serious crimes" with "trafficking in persons", earning "as a product of their crime" several millions of dollars, and befitting under the definitions of Article 2 and in the "laundering of the product of the crime" described by Article 6 of the Palermo Convention. Brazil meets all conditions and has the obligation to apply the Palermo Convention and its Annex on Trafficking in Persons, with regard to the case of Cuban physicians.

4

VENEZUELA

MORE CONCRETE ACTIONS AGAINST
VENEZUELA'S DICTATORSHIP

May 9, 2018

Venezuela's regime of organized crime is willing to indefinitely mock its people and the international community. The humanitarian crisis, narcotics' trafficking, the crimes, and the illegitimate and illegal hold of the political power that the Castroist Chavist system has produced and executes in Venezuela, have an impact on the whole region and the world. Democratic governments have the legal means to act by taking more concrete actions and end the danger Nicolas Maduro's dictatorship represents.

Venezuelans and the people who suffer the consequences of the Castroist Chavist dictatorships in the region are desperate and are already showing signs of being tired of further analysis, discourse, solidarity, and good intentions from democratic governments, international organizations and political leaders, all while the situation continues to deteriorate and worsens and the dictatorships close the cage of shamefulness in order to indefinitely remain in power.

Some important measures have been adopted by democratic countries such as; the United States, Canada, Costa Rica, Peru, and others, but these are not enough to stop the crimes the dictatorship commits daily in Venezuela. The only way to stop the dictatorship's crimes is to end the dictatorship itself.

In the current situation, International Law offers additional mechanisms to return freedom and democracy to Venezuela, without the need of having to resort to the use of force to restore international peace and security. Following are some suggestions of actions the world's democracies could avail themselves with regarding Venezuela's dictatorship:

- Expressly ignore Nicolas Maduro and his regime as the government of Venezuela, making him unable to continue representing it and acting on its behalf internationally. This would deprive the regime of the right to represent the state recognized by International Law.

- Withdrawal of ambassadors, such as what has been done by Costa Rica.

- Apply the Palermo Convention against Maduro and his accomplices for "substantial effects to other states". The international community cannot continue allowing Maduro to cover up his crimes with the argument that he is a government or with his ruse of sovereignty. The control of Venezuela by an Organized Crime's group and the daily commission of crimes that have an impact on the whole world *is not an internal matter but a matter of transnational organized crime.* Without taking narcotics' trafficking and crimes against humanity into account, the millions of Venezuelans who have been turned into forced migrants to Panama, Brazil, Colombia, Peru, Chile, Argentina, the United States, Mexico, Canada, Spain, and elsewhere, are living proof of this.

- Comply with the ruling of Venezuela's Supreme Justice Tribunal (the legitimate one that is in exile) who, with ample jurisdiction and competence, ruled for the prosecution and ineligibility of Nicolas Maduro to hold any civil service position and ordered the Bolivarian National Guard to serve notice and detain the dictator, and asked Interpol to issue a red alert. Thus far, the only one to acknowledge this Judicial Order has been the General Secretary of the Organization of American States (OAS).

- Suspend economic relations. It cannot be that while the United States, Canada, and other countries impose economic sanctions against Venezuela's dictatorial regime, other governments rotate their ambassadors as a clear sign of support due to their economic interests in Venezuela and the pressure exerted by the dictatorship.

- Ignore all acts and contracts of the dictatorship. Nothing internationally agreed to by the dictatorship ought to be acknowledged or recognized and shall not be recognized when democracy is restored.

- Nicolas Maduro's regime should be made ineligible to have the legal capacity to act on behalf of Venezuela at international organizations, coupled with the removal of representatives who it has already accredited.

- Identify and impose sanctions to non-democratic regimes who are partners of Venezuela's dictatorship in the region, regimes such as the ones in Cuba, Bolivia, and Nicaragua for their violations against international peace and security and their acts of interventionism.

- Urge the opening of prosecution proceedings against Nicolas Maduro and his accomplices at the International Court of Justice at The Hague, as a class action suit of international interest, respecting and abiding the purpose for which this organization was created.

- Open international pressure to Cuba's dictatorship because it is the one who organized, directs and sustains Maduro's regime.

NO INTERNATIONAL RECOGNITION TO VENEZUELA'S ORGANIZED CRIME

May 22, 2018

What dictator Nicolas Maduro and his regime insist in presenting as "elections" is a chain of serious crimes to misrepresent the popular sovereignty, sustain the narco-state, and guarantee himself impunity. The "organized crime group" that holds power has committed, and is willing to commit, whatever crime may be necessary to continue receiving the criminal benefits that have taken Venezuela to the on-going humanitarian crisis. What has happened in Venezuela are not elections but the supplanting of the electoral process by acts of the transnational organized crime group and the response that it merits is NOT to have the international recognition.

This is but a forced process that has been rigged to the convenience of the regime. A process that seeks to legitimize the illicit indefinite retention of political power that the Castroist Chavist system has by force in Venezuela. This is a process that seeks to hide the 80% of the Venezuelan population's rejection of Nicolas Maduro and his regime of shamefulness, intervention and dishonor, misrepresenting and falsifying a non-existent support.

It is an "iter-criminis" of an unending series of crimes of material and ideological falsehood, use of counterfeited instruments, illegal detentions, torture, assassinations, massacres, manipulation of the judicial due process with despicable rulings, supplanting of institutions of the government such as the Supreme Tribunal of

Justice, subjugation by force, bribery, narcotics' trafficking, armed robbery of the State's resources, thefts, extortions, falsification of the news, attempts against people's life and honor and against freedom of the press, forced migration of millions of citizens, threats for voting, electoral fraud, and many more crimes that reoccur using the power of the Government against the defenseless Venezuelan people.

Politics as "the activities ordained toward the common good" is an activity of service and public interest whose essence is for it to be legal, carried out within the framework of what is allowed according to justice, reason, and the common interest. On the other hand, delinquency refers "to the action of committing crime" and is something absolutely negative because it attempts against the common good, it causes harm and implies violence. Politics and delinquency are, therefore, antagonist concepts, they are the opposite of each other since one of the functions of politics is to avoid and prevent delinquency.

Nicolas Maduro ascended into power due to Hugo Chavez's death and did so by the imposition of Cuba's dictatorship that with Castro -the dictator- as its head controlled henceforth a project they labeled as the Bolivarian Movement, ALBA (America's People Bolivarian Alliance), 21stCentury Socialism, the Castroist Chavist system that has now evolved into the Transnational Organized Crime Group that still owns the regimes from Cuba, Venezuela, Nicaragua, and Bolivia.

The 21stCentury in Latin America has been branded -up to now- by those who presented themselves as populist politicians, socialists, progressives, from the new left, Bolivarian, anti-imperialist, promoters of the ALBA, followers of Hugo Chavez and Fidel Castro, who have retained power in Cuba, Venezuela, Bolivia, and Nicaragua. These same people who took power with Correa in Ecuador, with Lula and Rousseff in Brazil, with the Kirchner's in Argentina, with Insulza at the OAS, and with all the governments of the Petro-Caribe countries.

All these political leaders and their inner circle are now characterized by crime and corruption. The Castroist expansion project funded with moneys from Venezuelan oil and embezzled by Chavez -in another series of crimes- was always an anti-democracy and criminal undertaking.

Results and the objective reality have shown today that even if the Castroist Chavist system would have started with very altruistic political objectives for the common good of the nations, what has accomplished instead is; corruption, violence, organized crime activities never ever seen before, such as the "Lava Jato" and its "Odebrecht" scandal that has impacted the whole region, the "Nisman case" in Argentina, and what has began to be uncovered in Ecuador, or worse yet what is still covered up in Cuba, Venezuela, Bolivia, and Nicaragua whose Governments use power in order to remain unpunished.

Venezuela represents today -with what the regime calls "elections"- the most serious case of Organized Crime's activities. The response from democracies throughout the world subject to the Rule of Law is *not to recognize it*, in other words remove its condition of a subject of International Law. The opposite would be to accept the premise that crime creates rights.

RELEASING POLITICAL PRISONERS FROM JAIL BUT WITHOUT ANY TRUE FREEDOM OR LIBERTY

June, 7, 2018

Following the criminal acts committed before, during, and after the 20th of May's electoral supplanting to indefinitely continue the usurpation of power in Venezuela, Nicolas Maduro -true to Castroist methodology- now manipulates with the release of political prisoners from jail. It is the arbitrariness and cruelty of those who hold power and who play with the people's freedom and life, violating at their whim all human rights. A dictatorial maneuvering in the pursuit of political, economic, and propaganda objectives; to use these releases, but without any freedom or true liberty for those released.

It is very important for the victims, their families, and for society at large, that all political prisoners be released from the sinister Castroist Chavist's imprisonment centers in Venezuela and be returned to their homes. To the knowledge of everyone, those released, however, have not regained their freedom because the arguments, the manner and the objective of their release, are just as criminal as their original detention, prosecution, sentencing and imprisonment. The regime has power and when it releases prisoners with a "Commission for the Truth" of the usurped power, they are really demonstrating that they don't intend to give it up but are simply seeking to alleviate the national and international pressure that is about to depose them.

The detention of political prisoners -those who are now released- were criminal acts of extreme violence stemming from the political power, with false accusations, the misuse of the justice system as a mechanism for political repression and persecution, applying despicable rulings and laws, with Organized Crime's henchmen supplanting the functions of prosecutors and judges, who ruled despicable rules and sentences, and the misuse of the news media with fake news assassinating the victims' reputations.

Add to all of that the physical and psychological torture, solitary confinement, inhumane treatment -not only to the inmates but to their families as well- the perverse conditions of their imprisonment when they were jailed in areas with common criminals at the service of the dictatorship. A long list of common crime and crimes against humanity, violating the human rights of thousands of Venezuelans, impacting the entire population because the regime's end objective is to instill fear amongst the people, managing fear as an instrument of social control.

Nicolas Maduro and his Transnational Organized Crime's group carry out their activities in the style of Cuba's dictatorship and they do so with Cuban intervention. Venezuela with Chavez and Maduro, Bolivia with Evo Morales, Nicaragua with Daniel Ortega, and Ecuador with Correa carried out in the 21stCentury the cruelest violations of human rights of their people, as a repeat of what the Cuban people endures since 1959 when, under the banner of "revolution", organized crime took ownership of Cuba.

The Castroist regime has always had political prisoners and has always used them as exchange and transaction tokens for purposes of propaganda, and to obtain political and economic benefits. The Castro's have released political prisoners due to someone's influence or international pressure, and have always obtained benefits to, afterwards, continue filling their jails in order to have enough inmate capital as part of the human trafficking they practice with the prisoners. The case of Armando Valladares jailed for 22 years, declared a "conscientious objector" prisoner and released from prison by the regime due to the influence and request of France's president, is but one example of the Castroist methodology of using human trafficking as part of their "social control's methodology" with which they remain in power.

What is happening now in Venezuela is a replica of an already known story. A Castroist Chavist dictatorship, 21stCentury's Socialism of Organized Crime, it releases political prisoners but it does not free them. Even if they return to their homes, even if they are able to walk through the streets, there is no freedom. Even if some of those released political prisoners are able to go into exile that is not freedom either. Freedom is "the right of supreme value that ensures people's free determination"

There will not be freedom in Venezuela, Cuba, Bolivia, Nicaragua, Ecuador, and any country with political prisoners, while democracy does not return, even if those imprisoned are forced to leave prison and are able to go back and walk through the streets without any civil and political rights. There is no freedom in dictatorships and least of all in Organized Crime's regimes who have replaced politics with habitual and recurring crime. In Venezuela, they release political prisoners as a way to continue to remain in power.

COMPLY WITH THE RULING THAT DECLARES A CONSTITUTIONAL VOID IN VENEZUELA

July 10, 2018

Ratifying the "constitutional void in the National Executive Branch", Venezuela's Supreme Court of Justice (TSJ in Spanish) has issued, on July 2nd of 2018, *a ruling instructing, "the National Assembly from the Bolivarian Republic of Venezuela to proceed to fill the constitutional void of the Republic's Presidency until new presidential elections can take place".* To comply with this ruling means that the National Assembly designates a President of Venezuela, and for the international community once and for all to accept that Nicolas Maduro and his regime do not represent Venezuela and that whomever continues to have a relationship with, or be contracted by Maduro, does so at their own risk of disavowing the validity of any act of complicity with the Organized Crime's dictatorship.

In the "Castroist Chavist" dictatorial Venezuela, only two legal and legitimate institutions have survived and these are; the National Assembly, elected in the elections of December 6th of 2015 for a period of five years starting on January 5th of 2016, and the Supreme Court of Justice, designated and sworn in on July of 2017 "to do justice on behalf of the Republic".

The National Assembly has been turned into sort of a hostage of the dictatorship given that its members and political parties are; restrained in the dictatorship's cage, divided, persecuted, subjected to extortion and terror of the Castroist methodology. Some resist audaciously while others have been coopted into a "functional opposition". Maduro's regime with its criminal "Constituent Assembly" has rebuffed and supplanted the National Assembly, yet it continues recognizing its importance in order to manipulate the dialogue.

Venezuela's Supreme Court of Justice is comprised of 33 members elected for a twelve-year term, which initiated on July 21st of 2017. *Article 254 of Venezuela's constitution* establishes that *"the Judicial Branch is independent and the Supreme Court of Justice shall have functional, financial, and administrative autonomy".* Persecuted by the dictator Nicolas Maduro, however, the 33 members of the Supreme Court of Justice were forced into exile from where they continue to function, exercise jurisdiction and ample competency, with expressed international recognition from the Organization of American States (OAS), the European Parliament, countries such as; Panama, Chile, Colombia, and the United States (where its members now reside), from governments comprising the "Group of Lima" and international organizations.

The illegality and illegitimacy of Nicolas Maduro and his regime have been denounced politically and in the courts by the National Assembly and the Supreme Court of Justice, but the regime persists committing crimes to sustain its de-facto power, which have been exposed in four reports on Venezuela issued by the OAS' General Secretary that have created the "Almagro Doctrine".

They have been repudiated by the Venezuelan people in massive protests that have been responded with crime and massacres by the dictator and through their absenteeism at the electoral farce staged by the dictatorship this past May 20th. The resolution of the 48th General Assembly of the OAS on June 5thof 2018, has confirmed the regime's condition that has been corroborated by sanctions from the governments of Canada, the United States, and the European Union.

In this context and in strict utilization of the "Rule of Law" there is now the "legal order", the "legitimate legal instrument" to end Nicolas Maduro's dictatorial regime. We only have to comply with the ruling of July 2ⁿᵈof 2018 issued by Venezuela's Supreme Court of Justice:

- The governments of the Americas, the OAS, the European Parliament, the World Bank, the International Monetary Fund, all international organizations and institutions, have the obligation to suspend and immediately declare as *"inexistent, the representation of Nicolas Maduro and his regime"*. They are being served notice of the ruling, because the final part of said ruling dictates so.

- Venezuela's National Assembly has the obligation to designate a President of Venezuela, or a professional collegiate body, to perform those functions in order to have presidential elections that are *"free, fair, based on universal suffrage principles, and secret"*. The President, or professional collegiate body, designated by the National Assembly shall be immediately acknowledged and protected by the States of the Americas, the OAS, and the international community, replacing amply the supplanting functions that Nicolas Maduro and his regime exercise today.

NOT INTERVENING IS NOT AN ALIBI
TO JUSTIFY COMPLICITY

July 16, 2018

Mexico's President-Elect Andres Manuel Lopez Obrador and his nominated Secretary of Foreign Affairs Marcelo Ebrard, announced their return to the "Estrada Doctrine" in conducting foreign relations with "a policy of not getting involved in foreign matters that will seek not to meddle in conflicts such as the ones in Venezuela or Nicaragua". A mistaken political position that ignores existing International Law in whose context, "not intervening" and/or "the self-determination" are not an alibi of "complicity with Organized Crime's dictatorships".

The Estrada Doctrine was named after Genaro Estrada, Mexico's Secretary of Foreign Affairs and was published on 27 September of 1930. It states; "the government of Mexico does not grant accreditation because it considers this practice to be degrading since it, besides undermining the sovereignty of other nations, places these nations in a case in which their internal matters may be judged in any way by other governments who, in fact, assume an attitude of criticism in deciding favorably or unfavorably, over the legal capacity of foreign governments. The Mexican government limits itself only to keep or to remove its diplomatic representatives, anytime it deems this appropriate without judging precipitously, or after the fact, the right of the nations to accept, retain, or replace their governments of authorities".

The Estrada Doctrine proclaims to be founded on: the self-determination of the nations or their right to free determination that is "the right of a nation to decide on its own form of government, to accept, to keep, and to replace its authorities, to be freely structured without external interference", it is "the right of a nation to decide for itself" and not to intervene, meaning "that it is the obligation of the States to abstain from intervening, directly or indirectly, in the internal affairs of another State with the intent of affecting its will and obtaining its subordination."

The international legal standard of today is governed by –among other things- the United Nations Charter (UN) in existence since 24 October of 1945 that has as its purpose "the international peacekeeping and security"; by the Universal Declaration of Human Rights adopted on 10 December of 1948 with the fundamental objective "that Human Rights be protected by Law in order for people not to be compelled to the supreme recourse of rebellion against tyranny and oppression"; by the Charter of Bogota that created the Organization of American States (OAS) on 30 April of 1948; by the American Convention over Human Rights (Treaty of San Jose) of 22 November of 1969; by the Interamerican Democratic Charter (IDC) of 11 September of 2001.

The free determination of the nations and not intervening are not absolute principles as they were intended in 1930 when the Estrada Doctrine was published and are now applied within the framework of meeting "international obligations" among which the respect for human rights such as; the right of life, freedom, security, equality before the law, not to be subjected to torture, not to be arbitrarily detained, imprisoned, or exiled, to have free speech and freedom of the press, and many more, are preferred.

Democracy is a human right in the Americas. The Treaty of San Jose begins "recognizing the objective to consolidate, in this continent, within the framework of democratic institutions, a regime of personal freedom and that of social justice based on the respect for the basic rights of the people". Article 1 of the IDC establishes that "America's peoples have the right to democracy and their governments the obligation to promote and defend it".

Free determination is precisely what the people subjected to dictatorships *do not* have in Cuba, Venezuela, Nicaragua, and Bolivia where there is no respect for any of the basic components of democracy. With dictators who assassinate, massacre, imprison, exile, extort, who commit crime as the means to indefinitely sustain themselves in the government, these holders of power in narco-states; Raul Castro, Nicolas Maduro, Daniel Ortega, Evo Morales and their regimes is who Lopez Obrador is invoking the backward and out of date Estrada Doctrine to deal with, thus becoming in an accomplice and concealer?

5

BOLIVIA

THE 21ST OF FEBRUARY BOLIVIA ONCE AGAIN DEFEATED DICTATOR MORALES

February 27, 2018

In Bolivia, the 21st of February of 2016, the regime conducted a referendum to approve Evo Morales' indefinite reelection with a YES, the same tactic carried out in Venezuela, Nicaragua, and Ecuador. The Bolivian electorate, however, said NO and that day was recorded in the chronicles of history as "21F". What has transpired since then replicates what Hugo Chavez did after loosing his referendum of 2007. Evo Morales hatched a "despicable ruling" and his Constitutional Tribunal declared his human right to pursue and manipulate his "democratic" indefinite reelection. The 21st of February of 2018, with an overwhelming national civic work stoppage and massive demonstrations of protest, Bolivia once again defeated the coca grower dictator, warning him to abide by the original NO of 21F.

The destruction of democracy in Bolivia is marked by the toppling of democratically elected President Gonzalo Sanchez de Lozada on 17 October of 2003, followed by the granting of "amnesty" to the conspirators and plotters who passed from being the culprits to become the accusers, witnesses, and judges of those who they had toppled. In 2004 they supplanted the Law of Need of Constitutional Reform to counterfeit the constitutional validity of a "Constituent Assembly". Evo Morales was sworn to the presidency in January of 2006 for only one five-year term and with a specific constitutional prohibition of continuous reelection. He convened his constituent assembly and following a series of massacres, assassinations, imprisonments, exiles, and fraud, he eliminated the Republic of Bolivia and in 2009 established in its place the Plurinational State of Bolivia.

In the Plurinational State's constitution his craftiness led to the inclusion of a clause whereby a President may be consecutively reelected once. Immediately thereafter Morales called for elections and in the same year, 2009, was sworn in as the Head of the Plurinational State. Thus, and dating back to 2009, the separation and Independence of the branches of government disappeared. Morales took control of the Legislative Branch and designated and subordinated all members of the Judicial and Electoral Branches. The "Rule of Law" disappeared through a series of "despicable rulings" that violate Human Rights, such as the ruling that allows for the "retroactivity of the law" in order to persecute the leadership of political opponents. The judicially mandated political persecution was now officially institutionalized.

Evo Morales was supposed to hand over the Presidency in January of 2011 but, with the creation of a Castroist Chavist Plurinational State (a copy of the Bolivarian Republic of Venezuela) he consecutively reelected himself for the first time in 2009 with the obligation to hand over the presidency in January of 2014. With his control of the Judicial Branch, however, he hatched a ruling using the flawed argument that "since the Plurinational State of Bolivia was created in 2009, that year's election was his first, because his original election in 2005 to the extinct Republic of Bolivia does not count" and in 2014 was reelected consecutively for the second time for a third presidential term.

With a similar agenda already carried out in Venezuela, Ecuador and Nicaragua, as soon as he was sworn in for his third presidential term in 2014, Evo Morales declared the need of his indefinite reelection and with that in mind, called for a referendum election on 21 February of 2016. According to his estimates, this would be an easy victory especially when this referendum was taking place before the people began to feel an unavoidable and imminent economic crisis looming as a result of the corrupted narco-state government.

The defeat of the 21F referendum is for Evo Morales the loss of continuing to pursue any sign of simulation of democracy. It brought with it the generalized reaction of the people who, in a sustained and growing fashion and beyond political parties and beyond the figures of political party opposition with questionable independence from the regime, have made the compliance of the NO from the 21F a national objective, calling for "the restoration of democracy" and the "restitution of the Republic of Bolivia".

Bolivian people have again defeated Evo Morales and his regime this recent 21 February of 2018. This defeat has been so overwhelming that the regime has even contrived the use of fake news on the judicialized political persecution against former President Sanchez de Lozada.

Evo Morales is seen by Bolivians as a dictator and head of a de-facto government that becomes more illegitimate with the passing of time, a government that has foreign intervention from Cuba and Venezuela. The regime's efforts are focused on manipulating information, instilling fear in the population, pressuring and bribing sectorial, regional, and functional leaders to calm and demobilize the people and to collectively ascertain "United States imperialism as the foreign enemy" and "neo-liberalism and the right as internal enemy".

By the Bolivian people's decision, Evo Morales and his regime are but another of the Castroist Chavist dictatorships that are now falling apart.

THE SEA, THE HAGUE, AND THE DICTATORSHIP'S OTHER DECEPTIONS TO THE BOLIVIAN PEOPLE

Bolivia was deprived of her sovereign access to the sea, of a great portion of territory on the Pacific coast and all natural resources therein, through a war of invasion perpetrated by Chile in 1879 that also affected Peru –a Bolivian ally- who endured the occupation of Lima by Chilean forces and the loss of Arica. Bolivian maritime revindication is an unarguable right, it is the most important topic of national unity in Bolivia, but it also is the best instrument of political use. Evo Morales and his regime manipulate the topic of Bolivia's sovereign access to the sea, being discussed at The Hague, as another of the dictatorship's deceptions to the Bolivian people.

The armistice of the "Pacific War" was achieved through the Peace and Friendship Treaty of 1904 between Bolivia and Chile and through the Treaty of Lima in 1929 between Chile and Peru. This treaty in its complementary protocol establishes that *"the governments of Peru and Chile shall not be able to, without a prior agreement between them, cede to a third party the totality or part of those territories which, as prescribed in the treaty of this same date, remain under their respective sovereignty..."* This is why any solution with a sovereign access to the sea for Bolivia is a three party matter that must also include Chile and Peru.

There were a number of initiatives to resolve this matter; bilateral and multilateral talks, academic and political initiatives, international litigation, the intercession of organizations and states, mediation, backing from military dictatorships, direct, confidential, and secret negotiations. Bolivian president and intellectual Walter Guevara proposed a thesis calling for a "Tri-national Arica" as a solution for a territory to be shared among the three countries.

Ever since 1978, there are no diplomatic relations between Chile and Bolivia. Not having a sovereign access to the sea causes Bolivia the loss of at least 1% of its annual Internal Brute Production (PIB in Spanish). In the ensuing 139 year span, the country has been reduced to less than half of what it could have been with its own ports on the Pacific.

As a political propaganda effort with high costs, international advisors, expensive national staff, and abiding by the influence of the 21st century socialism, Evo Morales and his regime decided the Castroist-Chavist's use of Bolivia's maritime revindication to prop up and sustain his deteriorated image, cover up the crisis, and distract the people. Manipulating "the topic regarding which no Bolivian could be against", they sued in The Hague asking the International Court of Justice "to determine the obligation to negotiate" of Chile with Bolivia.

The Bolivian maritime cause has been reduced to be Evo Morales' regime's political instrument that he uses as another hot air balloon for the dictatorship, in the same way Maduro does in Venezuela. The objective reality, thus far, shows:

Bolivia's maritime revindication is NOT being litigated. This is NOT about the matter of essence. They are only asking "to determine the obligation to negotiate" of Chile with Bolivia. Something for which there has never been a need to enter into costly litigation.

The objective of the litigation is bilateral –Bolivia and Chile- on a matter that is tri-national in nature. Any solution or litigation must include Peru, as agreed in the Treaty of Lima of 1929.

If The Hague rules in favor of Morales' argument and Chile still refuses to negotiate, NOTHING happens!

If The Hague rules in favor of Morales' argument and Chile negotiates without any results, NOTHING happens! To negotiate does not mean to have an agreement and least of all to have a sovereign access to the sea.

Evo Morales with his narco-state is flooding Chile, Argentina, Brazil, and other countries, with cocaine. Chile's position on this matter is amply clear. Will Morales resign his Transnational Organized Crime relationship on this problem with Venezuela, Cuba, and Nicaragua, prior to entering into any negotiation?

The regime manipulates this "show" in order to; defuse the Bolivian people's rejection to Evo Morales perpetuation in power, to ignore the 21F referendum that clearly said NO to another term for Evo, to conceal his corruption and simulate –with a pilgrimage to The Hague- the existence of unity with complacent politicians, who were either deceived, or were recruited, and who knowingly became the dictator's choir.

Evo Morales has shown his trust on the influence over the judges in The Hague by his allies from Cuba, Venezuela, Nicaragua, Ecuador, and the countries from Petrocaribe, and the backing of Russia, China, Iran, and other "anti-imperialist" or "pro-terrorism" governments to accomplish "the order of dialogue or negotiation" and present it as "a historic victory". A pure and hardcore dictatorial strategy.

GONI AND SÁNCHEZ BERZAÍN WIN U.S. TRIAL- JUSTICE FOR BOLIVIAN DEMOCRACY

Washington, D.C. May 30, 2018

Today's decision by the Court brings to an end the trial over the difficult and painful days of September and October 2003 that interrupted democracy in Bolivia. The final judgment entered by the trial Court demonstrates that the administration of President Gonzalo Sánchez de Lozada and Minister Carlos Sánchez Berzaín acted in accordance with the law and without malicious intent. All those who worked in their government should be comforted by the Court's decision, which reaffirms what they always knew in their conscience.

The Court arrived at its decision after a careful and thorough analysis of the law and all the evidence presented at the trial. It found that the government of President Sánchez de Lozada and Minister Sánchez Berzaín acted within the law and in defense of innocent civilians. The Court further found that there was no plan or intent by their government to use lethal force against civilians. The evidence demonstrated that their government faced social upheaval in the midst of a serious economic crisis, seeking dialogue and the peaceful resolution of conflict, while many sought to destroy democracy.

However, President Sánchez de Lozada and Minister Sánchez Berzaín continue to mourn and feel the pain of those difficult days that their beloved country experienced in 2003, and share the hope that someday soon the whole truth of that period will be learned and accepted. This moment provides an opportunity to reflect on those sad days, to pray for those who were affected by violence, and to pledge to do everything possible to ensure that such tragedy never be allowed to happen again.

During the trial, we presented evidence about the economic, political and social reforms implemented during the two Constitutional and democratic administrations of President Sánchez de Lozada and Minister Sánchez Berzaín and the support they provided to the poor, indigenous populations, women, children and the elderly, in each case in accordance with the historical traditions of their party and their own personal and family history of public service.

We hope that the outcome of this trial reminds everyone how crucial justice is for democracy, and how essential it is to restore trust in democratic institutions. Bolivia deserves to, and must, regain its path to peace, progress and liberty.

Stephen D. Raber
Ana C. Reyes
Williams & Connolly

BOLIVIA-THE-HOMELAND-IS-CAPTIVE-THERE-ARE-NO-ELECTIONS-UNDER-A-DICTATORSHIP

July 3, 2018

An unequal fight is going on today in the Americas that is being fought by the people from Venezuela, Nicaragua, and Bolivia struggling to exit from the dictatorships created and controlled by the Castroist regime from Cuba, whose people have never stopped fighting against the tyranny since almost sixty years ago.

The fight by Venezuela's people is the most noteworthy and evident due to; the importance of the country who with its money and oil funded the re-creation of the Castroist craziness, and the magnitude of the humanitarian crisis that its dictator Maduro has taken it to. The Nicaraguan fight, almost ignored in these past few years, has turned nowadays into a crisis due to the decisive presence of the people on the streets protesting the brutal repression and crimes committed by its dictators Ortega/Murillo.

Bolivia's dictatorship uses a strategy to try to pass unnoticed and to continue simulating the existence of a democracy there and the achievement of inexistent economic gains, just as Venezuela and Nicaragua did until they could no longer hide their crises. Dictator Evo Morales forces and deceives Bolivians with an electoral process that only is a series of crimes to perpetuate himself in power. In this context, and on the basis of the experiences endured by the people from Cuba, Venezuela, and Nicaragua, I wish to send my compatriots the following message:

"Bolivia is under a dictatorship today. A look at the objective reality shows it to be so. There is no separation and independence of the branches of government because dictator Evo Morales controls all the power of the government, the Rule of Law is inexistent because the dictator has turned himself to be the undisputed law, there is political persecution and there is no freedom of the press. There are politicians who are persecuted, imprisoned, and exiled. There are NO chances of free, fair, and clean elections based on universal suffrage due to the control the regime exerts at every level, ranging from the people's personal identification, their registration into the electoral system, the rigging of the electoral system, the appointing of electoral authorities, and the removal of any possibility of free political association.

Through a referendum on 21 February of 2016, Bolivia ordered Evo Morales; not to run again in forthcoming elections and to leave the government. As an act of defiance and disobedience of the people's mandate, the dictator placed himself above the law and above the will of the people and continued to pursue the Castroist Chavist agenda -of which he is a part of- replicating, once again, what had been done in 2008 by Hugo Chavez in Venezuela, what had been done by the Ortega's in Nicaragua, and what dictator Nicolas Maduro has just done in Venezuela. Morales, with his Constitutional Tribunal and those despicable judges, got a ruling that enables him to run in the 2019 elections and that simply shows and proves but one more of so many crimes he has committed against our homeland, against Bolivians, and against freedom in our country.

This is why Bolivia, today, has one only objective which is to regain the homeland. This means to recover democracy and recover the Republic. To recover the conditions for democracy so that there may be free elections.

Reasons why, from my exile, I wish to make three proposals to the Bolivian people:

First, we must recognize the dictator for what he is. Point him for his corruption, for the economic crisis that he is taking Bolivia into, the same pathway of Cuba and Venezuela. Point him for the violations, abuse, and excesses that he commits that are crimes, because Bolivia's dictatorship is one more of those Transnational Organized Crime's dictatorships gathered around Venezuela and Cuba. Point him for the narcotics' trafficking that has caused that Bolivia nowadays be known as a "narco-state" within the international community.

Second, what I propose is a project for national unity that has nothing to do with ideology, political parties, personal, regional, or sectorial ambitions. It is about doing what was done in the decade of the seventies to regain democracy; regain democracy first and afterwards, vie for the power of government. To form an allegiance for democracy that will enable the majority of Bolivians to be against dictatorship and defeat it.

Third, I propose for everyone to have an awareness there are no elections in a dictatorship and that whomever plays along in the elections' games of Evo Morales for 2019, the only thing they are doing is that they are being used as pawns for the dictatorship and that when the dictatorship falls, such "functional opposition" will also fall with the dictatorship.

The message is very clear, there are no elections in a dictatorship and we Bolivians must unite in order to regain our homeland that is now captive"

AFTER THE DICTATORSHIP-BOLIVIA, A FEDERAL PARLIAMENTARY REPUBLIC

August 17, 2018

Upon reaching 193 years since the declaration of Bolivia's independence, Bolivians know their country is subjected to a dictatorship and are mobilized to recoup democracy, demand that the referendum of 21 Feb of 2016 which overwhelmingly said NO to Evo Morales whim to indefinitely remain in power, be abided by. The dictatorship has promoted national division, has eliminated the Republic, exacerbates presidentialism and uses centralism as a means of oppression and blackmail. In defeating the dictatorship, it is now necessary to; recoup the unity of the Bolivian people, construct democracy, and organize institutionalism with a new way of organizing the State and a different governmental system. It is time to organize society politically in accord to a reality that identifies Bolivia as a "Federal Parliamentary Republic".

The chieftainship, authoritarianism, political patronage, messianism and relativism in abiding by the law, are Bolivian and Latin-American cultural traits that lead to political instability and are useful in justifying the apparent solution with a greater ill that are dictatorships. Bolivia's history is a clear example of these traits that make out of politics the most needed and at the same time the most undesirable of activities.

Evo Morales' dictatorship in Bolivia is a criminal model of Cuban-Venezuelan transnational intervention that has setup mechanisms and nomenclatures in Bolivia with which the so-called 21st Century Socialism or Castroist Chavist system has sought to control the region. They have created new States in Venezuela and Bolivia and have setup others, such as Nicaragua and Ecuador, to have total and indefinite control of the government with despicable laws, judicialized political repression, control of the press, domesticated or controlled opposition, illicit enrichment, narcotics' trafficking, and the elimination of national independence with a antiimperialist discourse.

The same way that is in Cuba, Venezuela, and Nicaragua, the use of force is the backbone of the dictator Morales in Bolivia. Through a series of crimes, he has supplanted the Republic for a Plurinational State with the open objective of destroying the "Bolivian nation". In pursuing the destruction of the national identity, he has modified all the homeland's symbols, has changed the educational curriculum, has supplanted the values and principles of the Republic, has rejected the homeland's heroes, has revitalized and multiplied the fight between classes, sectors, regions, and cultures. He is in the process of changing the nation's Armed Forces' doctrine to turn them into dictatorial regime forces similar to those in Cuba, Venezuela, and Nicaragua.

Corruption is only surpassed by imagination, impunity has been institutionalized, and the country is now identified as a narco-state. Morales, who started out with the appearance of a populist president is the owner of lives and haciendas, supported by an inner circle of millionaires that he has created with corruption and narcotics' trafficking and their complicity. He controls all branches of the government and the country is his fiefdom that he is gradually turning over -at whim- to foreign powers. In order to take power and impose his regime, this Bolivian Castroist Chavist dictator has committed more than 20 bloody massacres that he covers up by attributing these crimes to the victims. Morales has been in power nearly 13 years and pretends to indefinitely continue in power.

In Bolivia there is no Government, there are no rights or justice, there are no checks and balances of a presidentialism system. To regain democracy, we must understand that this is about regaining freedom for Bolivians and the independence of their homeland. It is of utmost need now to address the basis that will construct the post Castroist Chavist dictatorship Bolivia as a "Federal Parliamentary Republic".

Republic is "a way of organizing a Government whose top authority is elected by the citizenry for a determined period". It is the opposite to unjust governments such as those of; despotism, tyranny, dictatorship. It is "the way of government governed by the common interest, justice, and equality". The Republic "is based on the eminence of the law and not the eminence of men". Contained within the concept of Republic are the components of democracy such as; the separation and independence of the branches of government and the existence of the Rule of Law. Bolivia has not been a Republic since 7 February of 2009.

Parliamentary democracy is a "governmental system" in which "the election of its Government or Executive Branch comes from parliament or Legislative Branch" that is elected by the citizenry. It has as its favorable features "the greater representation of the people" because it allows greater pluralism, "a greater response capability when confronting a governmental crisis" through its censorship vote, "greater stability with real political backing", and offers "a greater consensus in its decisions". Bolivia's municipal system has been parliamentarian since the enactment of the Popular Participation program and has worked well for over 24 years.

A Parliamentarian Republic is the state organized as a republic with a parliamentarian form of government. It separates the roles of the "Head of the State" from those of the "Head of Government" who performs executive tasks.

Federalism is a "political system that consists of promoting from the Central Government the autonomy of the regions, departments or states, who in the aggregate make up a nation". A "Federal Government" is "a sole institution comprised by several decentralized institutions with executive, legislative, and judicial branches of the Federation and of their own; these institutions cannot leave the Federation; there are two subordinated legal frameworks and there are exclusive, shared, and concurrent competencies of the Federation and of the regions, departments or states". The role of international relations, education and national defense must be Federal.

AMNESTY AS DICTATORSHIPS WEAPON
IS APPLIED IN BOLIVIA

October 5, 2018

The inexistence of the Rule of Law and the lack of separation and independence of the branches of government in Cuba, Venezuela, Bolivia, Nicaragua, and Correa´s Ecuador, is the medium for the total manipulation of the justice system that dictators convert into their instrument of political repression, subjecting victims to persecution, jailing, and exile. Castroist Chavist doctrine in the 21st Century has as a main component of its social control, the flawed processes with the appearance of trials against innocent people, with the objective of annulling or subjecting them. Closing this dishonorable loop, the dictatorships use "amnesty" as a weapon to continue the manipulation of the individual and popular will, as is now happening in Bolivia.

Amnesty is "the pardoning of certain types of crimes that extinguishes the responsibility of their authors". It deals with "the elimination of a crime´s penal responsibility". Its origin and concept comes from the Greek "amnesty/forgetting, pardoning", "without a memory of" to determine the "mutual and general forgetting of things past" and has –as one of its features- to be "a general standard that extinguishes the crime", different than the pardon that extinguishes only the serving out of the sentence. With the pardon the individual still is guilty but is absolved from serving out the sentence, with amnesty, however, the person no longer has a penal responsibility. Amnesty corroborates the existence of a crime and it legitimizes the accusation, because if there isn't a crime, there would be nothing to forgive.

In Cuba, Venezuela, Nicaragua, Bolivia, and Correa's Ecuador, a common practice was instituted for the dictator, or his cronies, to accuse citizens of crimes committed by the accusers or under the order of the accusers, or to falsely accuse them for inexistent crimes, or retroactively apply the dictatorships' new laws or procedures that did not exist in the past.

In innumerable cases, through public speeches registered in communications' media, the Castro's Chavez, Maduro, Correa, Ortega, and Morales have dished out accusations against political, civic, union, business, press, and religious leaders, ordering their arrest, prosecution, seizure of their assets, and have practically mandated their sentencing which –after the fact- the regime's "despicable judges" complied with by using the judicial system to carry out the ordered persecution.

Cuban, Venezuelan, Nicaraguan, Bolivian, and even some Ecuadorean political prisoners and exiles, are the result of judicial prosecution with false and manipulated accusations, without a legal due process, without the presumption of innocence, without the legal equality of the parts, without impartial judges, without probatory equality, without any legal guarantees that would enable these to be called "judicial prosecutions", VOID OF ANY LEGALITY.

Macabre orchestrations aimed at "assassinating the victims' reputation" that Organized Crime's dictatorships make against potential candidates, leaders, and defenders of freedom and democracy, with controlled publicity and a subjugated press. Examples of these theatrical sketches are the cases against Armando Valladares in Cuba, Leopoldo Lopez in Venezuela, Sanchez de Lozada or Las Americas Hotel or El Porvenir massacres in Bolivia, the prosecution for what happened on 30 September (30S) in Ecuador, and the current trial against members of the opposition and demonstrators for defending freedom in Nicaragua.

In this context, in Bolivia with over 1,200 political exiles, nearly 100 political prisoners, and thousands of politically persecuted, Evo Morales –with the argument of Bolivia´s maritime revindication, just announced the granting of amnesty for those he himself had ordered tried for corruption, namely; former presidents Carlos Mesa and Jorge Quiroga. Morales is manipulating the topic of Bolivia´s maritime revindication through its legal complaint filed at The Hague in order to ignore and disavow the Bolivian peoples´ decision rendered through a referendum election of 21 February of 2016 (21F), that prevents his reelection. The announced amnesty is but another shenanigan in that context.

History shows Morales, Mesa, and Quiroga to be very close: 1. Mesa granted amnesty to those who conspired and were the authors of the government´s overthrow in 2003, even up to now Morales is still protected by this amnesty and Quiroga publicly celebrated this break down of democracy. 2. The three of them carried out and approved the counterfeiting of the constitutional reform of 2004 by allowing for the constitution´s total reform through a constituent assembly with Law 2631, supplanting the text of the Law of Necessity for Reform. 3. They eliminated the Republic of Bolivia with the drafting of the Constitution of the Plurinational State of Bolivia and in collusion approved Law 3941 whose sole reading would prove the crime of "Treason to the Homeland" and others. 4. In the new Constitution of the Plurinational State, they expressly introduced the President´s consecutive reelection which was formerly expressly prohibited by the Republic´s constitution, something that has allowed thus far the perpetuation of Morales in power. 5. Morales, Quiroga, and Mesa presented the new Constitution of the Plurinational State as something "of national unity" and promoted it in the referendum election of 2009 that the regime won through fraud, while the people, Civic leadership, politicians and Governors of 6 out of 9 States were being massacred (Las Americas Hotel, El Porvenir, Cochabamba, La Calancha, and more), and were being persecuted, jailed and exiled.

What befits here, and what the unjustly accused, imprisoned, persecuted and exiled deserve is not amnesty but justice. This will only be possible with the return of democracy with its basic components, Rule of Law, separation of the branches of government, respect for Human Rights, and freedom of the press. The use of amnesty in Bolivia is but another weapon of the dictatorships amply applied there. Whomsoever accepts amnesty for crimes whomsoever never committed is legalizing the despicable accusations the regime falsely lashed out.

THE "COUP D`ETAT" THAT OVERTHROWERS CALLED "THE GAS WAR"

October 18, 2017

In October of 2003, Bolivia was celebrating 21 years of her return to democracy with a situation of extreme political violence around the city of La Paz, a situation that would ultimately give victory to conspirators bent on overthrowing the democratically elected President Gonzalo Sanchez de Lozada under the scheme of a "forced resignation". In one earlier attempt to overthrow the President in February of that year there had already been an assassination attempt against his life with tragic consequences and in August of the same year, the leader of the conspirators, Evo Morales, had broken the dialogue sponsored by the Catholic Church announcing, instead, that this was an all-out war. This violent conspiratorial process and the "coup d ètat" was labeled by the over throwers to be "the gas war".

In Bolivia, with the advent of the 21st century, political crises became more violent, more convoluted and more sustainable because instigators had resources and therefore the protests lasted longer, they were more aggressive and brought back the anti-imperialist and anti-capitalist discourse, they sought a regional confrontation, racial confrontation was added, and the reasons or causes of discontent were multiplied. The main sectors pursuing violent protests and demonstrations were the coca leaf harvesters for the illicit narcotics production and groups self-proclaimed as indigenous from the altiplano (Andean high plains) who were under the influence of guerrillas from Peru. It was the template for the Forum of Sao Paolo.

There had been a transcendental change; with the arrival of Chavez to power in Venezuela, the Castroist regime from Cuba -the only dictatorship in the Americas that after the breakup of the Soviet Union (USSR) and up to 1999 agonized within its "Special Period"- had received resources and had reactivated its interventionist apparatus, recreating its failed plan from the 60`s to expand its influence throughout the region. The Castroist subversives, guerrillas before, had been put into motion and would ultimately end up leading the Bolivarian Movement or ALBA, or 21st Century Socialism of the "Castroist-Chavist dictatorships".

The year of 2000 brought "The Water War" and the "Altiplano Blockade" against the government of President Banzer. In October of 2001, Evo Morales as the head of the Illicit Coca Leaf Harvesters Unions perpetrated what is known as the Massacre of Sacaba" during the government of Jorge Quiroga (who inherited the presidency for a year after the death of Banzer). The Massacre of Sacaba was Evo Morales` criminal attack against unarmed soldiers in which when injured soldiers were being evacuated by ambulance, the ambulances were attacked and the injured soldiers killed. For these crimes Evo Morales, who was a congressman from the lower house was legally tried and was ousted from Congress at the request of the opposition`s majority lead Sanchez Berzain, but entered into a Plea-Bargain agreement with the then Minister of Government Leopoldo Fernandez –today a political prisoner- who kept Morales from going to jail for 30 years.

The terrorist attacks of 11 September of 2001 in the United States dramatically changed the regional and global situation because the U.S. turned all her interest, resources, and means to the wars in Iraq and Afghanistan putting aside the agreements that had been made and promoted with Latin America on matters of the defense of democracy, the fight against narcotics trafficking and economic aid for development. Within this context, the coup d état of October of 2003 was largely ignored since it had not been neither the first coup against Sanchez de Lozada and Bolivian democracy, nor in the region where a president was overthrown in Argentina and two in Ecuador.

In January of 2003 Evo Morales organized blockades in the coca leaf harvest zones aimed to paralyze the government and encumber the people. He signed plea-bargain agreements when he was defeated only to immediately thereafter again conspire. The assassination attempt against the President in February of 2003 –investigated by the OAS- enabled to weaken the government while the conspirator effort grew and new demonstrations of violence and force started to flare up beginning with the massive kidnapping of over 1,000 national and foreign tourists that took place in Sorata, followed by the armed ambush against these tourists and the police and army forces who were escorting them back to La Paz.

Civilians, policemen, and Armed Forces` servicemen were attacked with firearms, snipers, and dynamite. The city of La Paz was under siege, the roadways and highways were blockaded. The constitutionally elected government applied lawful means to fulfill its obligation to protect the people, public utilities and services, strategic facilities, and private property, and soon thereafter the label "The Gas War" made its appearance as an alibi, accusing Sanchez de Lozada and his government to wanting "to sell gas to Chile" and wanting "to export gas to the United States through Chile". With the active participation of Peruvian subversives, members of the Colombian FARC, Castroist operators and local subversives, the over throwers applied the doctrine of the "revolutionary war" that calls for "causing killings in order to accuse the government for them".

With democracy now broken, they established the so-called October's agenda" pinpointing as objectives "the constituent assembly", "the nationalization of the oil industry", "the legal trial of the ousted government", "the elimination of traditional political parties", and others and a new de-facto period started in Bolivia with; amnesty decrees to ensure the impunity of the criminals of October of 2003, while Evo Morales now tried the defenders of democracy firing prosecutors who rejected to try for lack of legal cause, securing the passage of Constitutional Reform Law 2631 which falsifying the existing Constitution introduced the convening of a constituent assembly, superseding the already illegal text of the Constituent Assembly with Law 3941; electoral fraud in a referendum; rampant electoral fraud; disappearance of the Rule of Law; the assumption and control of all the branches of government; the indefinite reelection of Morales, and so forth.

After 14 years, the coup d'état that conspirators call "The Gas War" has produced; Evo Morales' Castroist-Chavist dictatorial regime, the disappearance of the Republic of Bolivia, over 20 bloody massacres, over a hundred political prisoners, over 1,200 political exiles, the disappearance of the freedom of the press, hundreds of new rich, a plurinational narco-state, Armed Forces who honor invaders such as Che Guevara, lies, infamy, and corruption.

BOLIVIA'S CASTROIST CHAVIST DICTATORSHIP CANNOT BE COVERED UP

November 7, 2018

Our treatment of Cuba, Venezuela, and Nicaragua as dictatorships is real, but Bolivia's dictatorship is a mockery of its true nature from every angle; analysis, news, and declarations. While there is an emerging consensus over the criminal nature of the regimes of the Castro's & Diaz-Canel, Maduro, and Ortega, the dictatorship of the Coca Growers' chieftain Evo Morales' seems to go unnoticed. The Castroist Chavist dictatorships from Cuba, Venezuela, Nicaragua, and Bolivia, all have the same features, methodology, and agenda, therefore Bolivia's dictatorship cannot remain covered up by misjudgment, omission or convenience.

The greatest propaganda efforts by the 21st Century Socialism's or Castroist Chavist's dictatorships has been, and still is, to feign democracy. Cuba's dictatorship has never had an option regarding this farce, but nevertheless it still insists appearing to present modifications to its dictatorial statutes manipulating them as "constitutional reforms". Venezuela's dictatorship has shed all of its disguise with the on-going humanitarian crisis and Nicaragua has left us no doubt of its dictatorial nature with the assassinations and violation of human rights that are taking place since this past April.

It is not that Venezuela's dictatorship exists only since a year ago and had made its appearance in the political scene with the hundreds of thousands of forced migrants, or that Nicaragua's dictatorship suddenly appeared committing crimes against the street protesters that started on the 18th of April. There is a dictatorship in Venezuela ever since Hugo Chavez was sworn in as President with his pledge to replace its "agonizing constitution" and then forged an alliance with Castro and harnessed all power to himself. Nicaragua is a dictatorship since, at least, 2009 a year in which Daniel Ortega made "inapplicable" Constitutional Articles 147 and 148 that prohibited the continuous reelection of the President of the Republic."

Evo Morales' regime in Bolivia is a dictatorship, is part of a Castroist Chavist Transnational Organized Crime network, is a threat to the world and violates Bolivians' human rights and individual freedoms. More than 20 massacres with over 100 dead in the city of Cochabamba, the town of El Porvenir in the Pando department, Las Americas' Hotel in the city of Santa Cruz, La Calancha in the city of Sucre, and the Yungas province in the department of La Paz, and elsewhere in mining towns, offer unquestionable proof. This is also ratified by on-going political persecutions that use the Judicial Branch with over 80 political prisoners and over 1,200 political exiles certified by the United Nations' Refugee Agency.

In January of 2019, dictator Morales will have reached 13 years of continuous power despite the fact that he was elected for 5 years without a right to be continuously reelected. Morales has counterfeited the constitutional reforms of 2004 and in a partnership with Carlos Mesa introduced the "Constituent Assembly" to totally revamp the constitution even though the Republic's Constitution only allowed for a partial reform. Along with the same group of "Valencia's Constitutionalists" that operated in Venezuela, Cuba, and Ecuador, he has falsified the approved constitutional text by the already illegal Constituent Assembly; has replaced the Republic of Bolivia with his "Plurinational State", has voided all power in all democratically constituted institutions, has changed their name, in order to conduct purges and get rid of legitimate magistrates; has committed electoral fraud in elections, referendums and more.

Morales' Plurinational State's Constitution, in existence since 2009 – replicating that of Cuba's- consecrates the "retroactivity of the law" violating the Universal Declaration of Human Rights.

Internationally, Evo Morales promotes coca and cocaine, as evidenced by his speech at the UN in April of 2016. He has increased the harvesting of illegal coca from 7,410 acres in 2003 to a whopping 172,900 acres with a production of cocaine that is now flooding Brazil, Chile, Argentina, and operates an official narcotics' trafficking network with Venezuela using military airplanes, as proven by journalist Leonardo Coutinho in his writing "Hugo Chavez or a Specter".

To get a firm foothold for his "Criminal Plurinational State" just as Venezuela and Ecuador with Correa did, he has expelled the US Ambassador and the DEA, breaking international counternarcotic agreements. He has also created and operates "ALBA's Anti-Imperialist Military School" located in the city of Santa Cruz with instructors from Cuba, and Iran, amongst others. He has ended freedom of the press and his control of the media allows him to continue selling a counterfeited economic success, and a "false indigenous image" that does not speak any of the indigenous languages. He has fiercely repressed the true indigenous peoples of the TIPNIS to rob from their natural reserves with the expansion of his illegal coca harvesting.

THE MOST RECENT POLITICAL PRISONER IN BOLIVIA IS A 26-YEAR-OLD CONSTRUCTION WORKER

November 14, 2018

Anyone who insists to continue believing the farce that Evo Morales' regime is an imperfect democracy, attempts to distance it from the undisguisable dictatorships from Cuba, Venezuela, and Nicaragua, now with the increase of political prisoners in Bolivia, has one additional proof of the dictatorial nature of this regime. An ordinary citizen who shouted "Bolivia said NO" to Evo Morales in the city of Potosi is now under arrest and is being prosecuted by the Castroist Chavist system.

The most recent political prisoner in Bolivia is a young Bolivian construction worker of 26 years of age, Moises Montero Chambi who now faces up to 10 years in jail for shouting a truth established by the majority of Bolivians through a constitutional referendum.

Each 10th of November, the anniversary of the foundation of the Potosi Department is celebrated as a remembrance of its uprising for freedom in 1810. The capital of the Potosi Department is "the Imperial Villa of Potosi" worldwide known for the riches of its "Cerro Rico de Potosi" where the world's greatest silver mine, since the 16th century is located, a source of huge wealth for the Spanish Crown in the colony and a very important source of support to the nation's economy.

It is customary that in the celebration of the anniversary of each of the Bolivian Departments, there be a Presidential visit when he announces forthcoming "gifts" for the Department celebrating. This practice, in Evo Morales' regime, has been institutionalized by the centralism and overdependence on the President's power, exacerbated by the fact that every project or expense of public funds must pass through the cycle; decision, control, and inauguration by the President, process that affixes his name to them, and demands political retribution -or payback- for such projects or expenditures which, in general, are notorious for being of poor quality, having cost overruns, and resulting from corruption.

This past November the 9th, the Head of State arrived at the city of Potosi where a young man shouted at him "BOLIVIA SAID NO", reason why the young man was immediately detained with an initial argument claiming that he had shouted such unprecedented phrase, poured a glass of water, and had hurled a bag with coca leaves at the President attending a Departmental Assembly meeting. Afterwards, the official version removed the glass of water and the bag of coca leaves because their detainee was never ever even near the dictator.

Bolivia is living today a growing social and political crisis generated by Evo Morales' persistence to remain indefinitely in power. Morales climbed to Bolivia's presidency in January of 2006 for a five-year term and without the possibility of continuous reelection, but despite of that he has already remained 13 years in power.

Using the Castroist Chavist mold, previously applied in; Venezuela with Chavez, Ecuador with Correa, and now being applied in Nicaragua with Ortega, he supplanted the Republic's Constitution in order to force the formation of a Constituent Assembly, he is responsible for having caused over 20 bloody massacres to assassinate, imprison, and exile those defenders of the Republic and after supplanting the text of his own Constituent's constitution, he created in 2009 the "Plurinational State of Bolivia" that allows him to have total control.

The constitution of his "Plurinational State" allows Morales a one-time consecutive reelection, argument he used immediately calling for elections the same year (2009) and being sworn-in as the Head of the Plurinational State in January of 2010 for five-years. In 2014, however, he used a subservient Constitutional Tribunal so that with one ruling, it authorized his second consecutive candidacy using the flawed argument that "since the Plurinational State was founded in 2009, his election for the former Republic of Bolivia did not count."

With the use of every trick in the book, massacres, corruption, and other crimes, Morales, in January of 2015, was again sworn in as Head of the State for another five years and immediately thereafter called for a Bolivian people's referendum to allow for his indefinite reelection. The referendum election took place on 21 February of 2016 (21F) and BOLIVIA SAID NO. This meant that by popular mandate, the Bolivian people wanted to put an end to the forced chain of crime and that Evo Morales can no longer be a candidate and to simulate electoral victory through fraud and more crime.

But, just as Hugo Chavez had done and Nicolas Maduro does in Venezuela, and Ortega in Nicaragua, Evo Morales is already in an electoral campaign to simulate his reelection in 2019, reason why he obtained yet another "despicable ruling" from his Constitutional Tribunal who, going over the head of the people's popular mandate and its own constitution, has ruled that Morales has "the human right to an indefinite candidacy".

In Bolivia there are close to 80 political prisoners and over 1,200 political exiles, all accused and prosecuted by the dictatorship's judicial system that retroactively applies laws, does not recognize the right to one's own defense, is comprised by prosecutors and judges that are mere operators of the regime, are not impartial, and are not qualified. It is a copy of the Castroist system that has turned justice into an apparatus for the repression and the assassination of those defenders of freedom and democracy.

It is in this context that Moises Montero Chambi a citizen of 26 years of age, for shouting BOLIVIA SAID NO, has been formally charged for the crime of "attempting against the President and other Dignitaries of State", as prescribed in the dictatorship's Article 128 of the Penal Code, with a sentence from 5 to 10 years in jail. He is the most recent political prisoner and the dictatorship now offers him to option to confess to a crime he did not commit, apologize to the dictator, obtain a less harsh sentence and regain his freedom, or follow the path of those Bolivians who have died in jail or are still there.

BOLIVIA FORCED INTO EXERCISING THE SUPREME RIGHT OF REBELLION

December 13, 2018

Applying Cuba's screenplay carried out in Venezuela and Nicaragua, Evo Morales just finished manipulating his regime's Supreme Electoral Tribunal forcing it to rule him as a viable candidate for the 2019 elections and afterwards, thus imposing his indefinite reelection. Bolivians no longer have any doubts they are subjected to a dictatorship, while the regime increases its intimidation, control of political actors, and control of the press. The counterfeiting of democracy has become obvious and Bolivia's people are being forced to exercise their supreme right of rebellion against tyranny and oppression.

The right to "the supreme recourse of rebellion against tyranny and oppression" is a natural and legal right recognized in the Universal Declaration of Human Rights. Aleksandar Marsavelski summarizes this as "the right of peoples facing those governing who are from an illegitimate origin or those who -having a legitimate origin- have transformed into illegitimate in the course of their government, that authorizes civil disobedience and the use of force in order to topple and replace them with governments who have legitimacy".

The right to rebellion was first proclaimed by Plato and backed up by Saint Thomas de Aquino. It is included in the Declaration of Independence of the United States that after declaring the right "to life, liberty and the search for happiness" it establishes that "in order to guarantee these rights amongst men, governments who derived their legitimate power from the consent of those governed are instituted; and that anytime a form of government becomes destructive of these principles, the people have the right to reform or abolish it and to institute a new government that is based on said principles…"

Article 35 of the Declaration of Rights of Men and the Citizenry of the French Revolution states that "when a government violates the rights of the people, insurrection is, for the people and for each of its sectors, the most sacred of rights and the most indispensable of duties". All Constitutions by recognizing that "sovereignty rests with the people and that its performance is delegated" back up the right to rebellion.

The 21st Century Socialism, or Castroist Chavist doctrine applies the methodology of supplanting the democratic order with despicable laws "to legally violate" Human Rights, and individual basic freedoms and to commit all type of crimes with impunity. What is taking place in Bolivia is only the closing of a process that started in October of 2003 with the toppling of a democratically elected Constitutional President through a coup d'état using the fallacious argument of defending the country's oil resources that topplers labeled "the Gas War". They, afterwards, supplanted the Constitution and eliminated the Republic of Bolivia through an irritant "Constituent Assembly".

The call for the "indefinite reelection" of Evo Morales caps an ongoing fifteen year "iter criminis" period and starts another of indefinite duration and with unforeseen consequences. Replicating Chavez and Maduro in Venezuela and Ortega in Nicaragua, Evo Morales who ascended into power for a five-year period that had to be concluded in 2011, will now celebrate 13 years in power and has everything arranged to yet once more "win elections that have been orchestrated to meet his needs". He will do so through the commission of a chain of crimes that range from; the Constitutional supplanting, the disappearance of the Rule of Law, the garnering of all power, the disavowing of the popular will expressed through the 21 February of 2016 referendum (21F), down to electoral fraud through the control of the citizenry's identification, voter registration, publicity, the press and of all officials who should be impartial but that now comprise "the criminal Group of 6" at the service of the dictator.

The situation is so dire that Evo Morales as "electoral dictator" controls even the opposition's candidates who must now go through a process of Primary Elections in order to consummate the disavowing of the 21F mandate in an environment that simulates democracy. Bolivian leaders now have the urgent challenge of deactivating the dictator's electoral farce by making the truly democratic candidates to abandon the electoral race, calling it out by what it really is, because those who stay in the race will do so as functional props and accomplices to legitimize the dictator.

Evo Morales' dictatorship and Cuba's and Venezuela's Castroist Chavist intervention in Bolivia force Bolivians to exercise their supreme right of rebellion. Protesting Bolivians shout "Bolivia is not Venezuela" and I hope they are right, because just some years ago Venezuelans shouted "Venezuela is not Cuba".

LETTER FROM CARLOS SÁNCHEZ BERZAÍN TO PRESIDENT JAIR BOLSONARO

26 December of 2018

Mister President:

I have the honor to contact you for the purpose of asking you to kindly review and revoke the invitation extended to the Head of the Plurinational State of Bolivia to your swearing in as the President of the Federative Republic of Brazil.

What motivates my request to you is that similar invitations to the Heads of State from Cuba, Venezuela, and Nicaragua have been withdrawn, while the Bolivian regime, that incurs in violations as severe or even more serious and openly acts against Brazil and its future government, remains invited. Please indulge me in the following reminder.

1.- Regarding the violation of the Bolivian people's freedoms –in a nutshell and to sum it up- Evo Morales leads an Organized Crime's regime.

1.1.- He has extinguished the Constitution of the State of Bolivia through counterfeiting and deliberate acts, has eliminated the Republic of Bolivia supplanting it with a Plurinational State. In Bolivia, today, Human Rights are violated as part of the methodology for political control introduced and controlled by Cuba and Venezuela, there isn't separation and independence of the branches of government, there is no Rule of Law, there is political persecution using the judicial branch that has been institutionalized and that as a consequence there are over one hundred political prisoners and more that 1,200 political exiles (most of these as refugees in Brazil). Morales has committed over 20 massacres, such as the ones at; El Porvenir, Hotel Las Americas, Cochabamba, La Calancha, with 89 people assassinated.

1.2.- Elected for one 5-year term, without the right to a consecutive reelection, this coming January he will celebrate 13 continuous years as the Head of State with the title of President and the performance of a dictator. To govern all of this time, besides committing the crimes mentioned in the previous paragraph, Morales now pretends to be a candidate in the forthcoming elections of 2019 in order to indefinitely remain in power and pretends to ignore the results of a referendum that he himself called to be held on 21 February of 2016 (21F) through which Bolivian people said NO to any more of his reelections. Availing himself of a despicable Constitutional Tribunal ruling, manipulations of the Supreme Electoral Tribunal -both under his control- Morales has been enabled to be a candidate. Today in Bolivia there are more than 200 Bolivian citizens undergoing a hunger strike and popular demonstrations demanding that he abide by the results of the 21F referendum.

1.3.- He has turned Bolivia into a narco-state, increasing illegal coca cultivation from 7,413 acres in 2003 to more than 123,550 acres, while also and unnecessarily increasing the cultivation of legal coca for local consumption. Morales is the perpetual leader of the Illicit Coca Cultivation Unions in the tropical area of Cochabamba known as Chapare, these are his political base and they have practically integrated to the coca-leaf cultivation, the production of cocaine. In his book "Hugo Chávez o Espectro" Brazilian journalist Leonardo Coutinho documents the existence of a "cocaine's aerial bridge" involving the official air traffic between Bolivia and Venezuela and the "narco-Bolivarianism" that has Brazil as one of its victims.

1.4.- Bolivian Senator Roger Pinto was a refugee at the Brazilian Embassy in La Paz for 15 months, politically persecuted by the Morales' regime. Thanks to the humanitarian actions of Brazilian Diplomat Eduardo P. Saboia, Senator Pinto was able to flee to Brazil where he was granted Political Asylum. Roger Pinto died exiled in an "aviation accident" but he has left a very clear picture of Morales' violation of Human Rights in Bolivia, even against a sitting Senator.

2.- Evo Morales, beyond ample ideological affinity with the group defeated in the elections in which the Brazilian people elected you as their President, is part of the transnational project known as "The Forum of Sao Paolo". Here are some facts that I would like to mention:

2.1.- Everything mentioned in the paragraphs above and more, has been made and sustained within the framework of "The Forum of Sao Paolo" and the "Caracas-Havana" axis that with the label of ALBA, Bolivarian Project, or 21st Century Socialism and now simply as "Castroist Chavist" doctrine, has -until recently- controlled Latin America.

2.2.- Evo Morales has humiliated the Bolivian Armed Forces by vindicating and erecting monuments of Che Guevara who invaded my country, has called Fidel Castro "his dad", is an avowed follower of Hugo Chavez an unrelenting defender of Cuba's, Venezuela's and Nicaragua's dictators and this is how he casts his votes and that of Bolivian representatives at all international forums. He sustains Cuba's "Slave Physicians" program, thousands of whom are in Bolivia and has publicly offered employment to any of these physicians who abandoned Brazil's "Mais Medicos" program.

2.3.- Regarding the topic of corruption, the "Lava Jato" scandal has been and continues to be carefully covered up -until now- in order to avoid revealing Evo Morales' involvement. Only as an example, please allow me to remind you that Luis Ignacio Lula da Silva personally promoted the construction of the highway that violates the indigenous and natural reserve known as "TIPNIS" in Bolivia. The little bit of information that Bolivian public opinion has on the case of the Bolivian Lava Jato comes from cases investigated and revealed in Peru. Evo Morales and his regime are responsible for the death of Jose Maria Bakovic, Director of the National Highway Service who was harassed all the way to his grave to give-in to corruption. It is urgent, Mr. President, that all matters relative to; contracts, cost overruns, bribes, and the involvement of officials from Bolivia and Brazil, ever since the Worker's Party (PT) took the government, be made openly public, because if the delivery of the results of investigating these matters continues to be from government to government, Evo Morales will continue covering them up.

2.4.- The increase of the production of coca and cocaine as Evo Morales' regime's state policy has flooded the region with drugs, turning Brazil into the most impacted country due to its lengthy border with Bolivia and its large population. The increase in the prevalence of cocaine consumption in Brazil, along with the ensuing increase in crime and the enrichment of dangerous criminal groups, threatens Brazilian stability and comes from narcotics' production in territory controlled by Evo Morales who, at the same time and as a declared friend, has sustained Colombia's FARC sponsored by Cuba, another source of direct threat and by means of the axis that Venezuela has been turned into.

Undoubtedly, Mr. President you know these facts and many more. You also know that the Castroist Chavist dictatorial regimes in the Americas are; Cuba, Venezuela, Nicaragua, and Bolivia, that with the same mechanisms and crimes formulated, coordinated, and executed between themselves, oppress their people and threaten democracies such as Brazil's.

Bolivia's peoples are fighting for their freedom and to recover democracy. Evo Morales is a dictator who has no intention of leaving the government because he needs impunity and acts under a common strategy with Cuba, Venezuela, and Nicaragua, as was proven by the recent meeting of dictators Castro-Diaz Canel, Maduro, Ortega, and Morales in Havana on the 14th and 15th of this month under the umbrella of "ALBA-TCP".

For three dictators; Cuba's, Venezuela's, and Nicaragua's, respectively, not to be invited to the swearing-in of Brazil's democratically elected president, while Evo Morales is invited will be tantamount to a reward and great benefit for the attending dictator who will continue simulating a legitimacy of a democracy that is non-existent.

Respectfully,

Carlos Sanchez Berzain

6

DEMOCRACY

KNOW THEIR STRATEGY, DEFEAT DICTATORSHIPS, AND THEN ELECTIONS

January 16, 2018

There are important advances in the fight to recoup democracy from the hands of Castroist-Chavist dictatorships, but these regimes commit and are most willing to commit all types of crime in order to remain in power. The objective conditions of their governments enable us to know the dictatorships' strategies, but it is vital to remember that, first of all, the dictatorships must be defeated, so that afterwards -in democracy- power can be disputed through free and fair elections.

To regain democracy in Cuba, Venezuela, Bolivia, and Nicaragua is a national challenge for each nation, for each country, with their own important local peculiarities. The common denominator, however, is that they confront a transnational dictatorial system of organized crime stemming from the Castroist "internationalism" of the sixties, recreated and structured to continually violate all Human Rights with a standardized strategy of de-facto regimes.

To keep in power the Castro's in Cuba, Maduro in Venezuela, Evo Morales in Bolivia and the Ortega's in Nicaragua the regimes apply certain common concepts such as; "fear", "force", "identify and divide the internal enemies", create the existence of "external enemies in order to present themselves as victims", "politicize and control information". The Cuban dictatorship has been doing this for over five decades, not without fright and risk, but up to now with success.

Fear is an essential component of dictatorships, this is why they kill the "Rule of Law" and supplant it with the "Rule of the State" with "despicable laws" to enable them to persecute, imprison, dishonor, and wrest the property of, citizens. This is what the new Penal Code of Evo Morales seeks and why, right now, the Bolivian people are rejecting it, this is the same code that is already lawfully enforced in Cuba, Venezuela, and Nicaragua.

The force needed to sustain these regimes of fear is based on the control of the military and police hierarchies until the indoctrination and militancy of all members is achieved, a purpose for which the component of fear is also applied, turning them into institutionalized violators of Human Rights and in patsies when there is a need to coverup the regime. This is exactly what happened in Cuba when General Ochoa was executed by a firing squad, and what is happening in Venezuela with General Baduel, and many more. Force is also exerted through irregular groups, gangs, thugs, experts of "Castroist internationalism", criminal groups such as the FARC from Colombia and, if necessary, through the help from terrorism.

The internal enemy is the nation, society, political groups and their leadership, who have to be divided, co-opted, or eliminated. This is why the topics of confrontation are multiplied and go beyond racism, regionalism, gender, generational, sectorial, functional, anything and everything that will divide society, its institutions, and subject them to dispute. Currently in Bolivia, the dictatorship of Evo Morales that does not acknowledge the Bolivian nation as the identity for all Bolivians, is intensifying racial confrontation, attempting to divide -through lies and fear- the people who since the National Revolution of 1952 advanced in unity, in diversity.

The foreign or external enemy is the "North American imperialism" with which dictatorships justify all of their abuse, corruption and crime, even narcotics trafficking as Evo Morales did at the U.N.

The foreign enemy is useful in order to blame the United States for all disastrous results from the organized crime that holds political power, such as what the Castro's have done for many years and now Maduro, Morales, and their thugs do.

Every criminal act violating Human Rights that is committed by the dictatorship is "politicized" and presented with "control of the information" and propaganda. Nowadays the regimes from Cuba, Venezuela, Nicaragua, and Bolivia claim "the right" conspires, pays, and wants them toppled, attributing to themselves the position of being "leftist", socialist, and communist, when -in reality- they are criminal "fascists" whose sole ideology and objective is the total and indefinite control of power along with their illicit enrichment.

With its strategy known, it has been shown that the fight against dictatorship is not a confrontation of the right against the left because everyone wants to recoup democracy, as was shown by the reorganization of Bolivia's National Committee for the Defense of Democracy (CONADE in Spanish), that was originally created to restore democracy in the seventies and that has been recently reactivated a few days ago against Evo Morales. All united against the dictatorship, and then elections in democracy.

MESSAGE TO LULA AND HIS ASSOCIATES- "THE LAW IS ALWAYS GOING TO BE ABOVE YOU"

January30, 2018

The ruling issued by the Federal Regional Tribunal from Porto Alegre, Brazil, unanimously ratified the guilt of Luis Inácio Lula da Silva for "passive corruption and money laundering" with the construction company OAS in the "Lava Jato" scandal and extended his sentence from 9 to 12 years of jail. It is a message to Lula's associates in the regimes of Cuba, Venezuela, Bolivia, Nicaragua, Ecuador, and others. Judge Leandro Paulsen asserted "Let it be understood by all that … without regard of how high the pedestal that puts you in power may be, THE LAW will always be above you."

There is Rule of Law when "the law is above those who govern, and not the other way around, and because of that the law is equally applied amongst all citizens". This is about recognizing that "any power be limited by law that not only conditions its manner of enforcement but also its content". One of the signs of the existence of the "Rule of Law" is the separation and independence of the branches of government given the fact that both; the Rule of Law and the separation and independence of the branches of government, are essential components of democracy. This is why the decision of the Brazilian judges in Lula's case, is a clear demonstration of the strength of democracy in Brazil, something wished for and even envied for, by many nations of the region.

Extending Lula's sentence is a "red flag" to the corruption network established in Brazil and spread throughout the Americas that began with the "Forum of Sao Paolo" and its political birthing of the 21st Century Socialism, known today also as "Castroist-Chavist". During his government, Lula received from the OAS construction company a triplex apartment in the resort of Guarujá, valued at $1.2 million dollars in exchange for OAS contracts with Petrobras such as the Abreu e Lima refinery that Lula inaugurated together with Hugo Chavez.

Lula's case is part of the "Lava Jato" scandal, the greatest transnational political corruption scandal, a network of organized crime established with political objectives from the "Forum of Sao Paolo" to enrich Castroist-Chavist governments who -with those illicit funds- manipulated elections and communications media, violated and violates human rights and destroyed democracy in Venezuela with Chavez and Maduro, in Ecuador with Correa, in Nicaragua with the Ortega's, in Bolivia with Evo Morales, in Argentina with the Kirchner's, and in several of the Petro-Caribbean countries, under the control of the Castro's Cuban dictatorship.

The investigation into "Lava Jato" revealed that "members of the Brazilian government (Lula) spread this network of "under the table" payments so that the larger construction companies of that country be awarded sizeable contracts throughout Latin America". The case that is most widely known is that of Odebrecht, but around fourteen other Brazilian construction companies are under investigation. This is the case of the OAS construction company in Bolivia with projects and contracts publicly promoted by Lula and Evo Morales, such as the construction of a highway that encroaches into and destroys a protected indigenous reserve known as the "TIPNIS" in order to expand the illicit cultivation of coca.

Lula's sentence is a clear signal to the chief of the monumental mechanism "for the internationalization of corruption" under the Cuban's dictatorial doctrine who schemed so that "never again be lacking money to pursue revolutionary efforts" which is nothing more than to destroy democracy. Besides snarling the regimes of Venezuela with Chavez and Maduro, Nicaragua with the Ortega's, and Bolivia with Evo Morales that are nowadays known as dictatorships, this corruption touched and corrupted practically the entire region, as was revealed in the cases of the Kirchner's in Argentina, Toledo, Humala and others in Peru, the higher echelons of Correa's regime in Ecuador that still continue to protect Correa, the cases of Panama, Dominican Republic, Mexico, and others.

Brazilian judges have concluded that "there is more than reasonable proof that the former president (Lula) was one of the masterminds, if not the main one, to create a vast corruption network". Lula's legal defense stands no chance, this is why it has focused on politicizing the trial thus far to no avail due to the existence of the "Rule of Law", the seriousness and independence of the judges, and the weight of the proof. Judge Joao Gebran Neto, a member of the court that extended Lula's sentence, denied an alleged persecution by the Judicial Branch asserting that "the Judicial Branch cannot be guided by the political consequences of this type of trials."

CORRUPTION, UN-GOVERNABILITY AND DEMOCRACY THAT WORKS IN PERU

March 28, 2018

In Peru Pedro Pablo Kuczynski (PPK) was elected in a second round of voting as a weak president, riding on the premise to prevent, at all costs, Keiko Fujimori's election to the presidency. His election resulted in a fragile government with a minority of seats in congress, functioning within a very bureaucratic presidentialist system. The forum of Sao Paolo with Lula da Silva at its head and roughly 15 construction companies, amongst which Odebrecht stands out, have left their stain of corruption throughout the Americas. These two elements; ungovernability and corruption, have just led to PPK's demise, but at the same time have shown a democracy that works in Peru.

With the revelations of the "Lava Jato" corruption scheme, almost all of Latin America's governments have been implicated. Odebrecht is one of the Brazilian companies implicated in the Forum of Sao Paolo's criminal network implemented by Lula da Silva with the dictators Fidel Castro and Hugo Chavez with the payment of millions of dollars in bribes. Yet to be investigated are contracts, construction projects, overpricing, bribes, and corruption of the rest of the suspected Brazilian construction companies such as; OAS, Queiroz Galvao, Andrade Gutierrez, Camargo Correa, Mendez Junior, UTC Engineering, and others.

The reaction from those countries implicated in the "Lava Jato" scandal has been of three types:

Fight Against Corruption. Countries with democracy, separation and independence of the branches of government, existing "Rule of Law" and freedom of the press, have opened vigorous investigations and have decisively moved forward. Brazil has impeached and removed President Rousseff, has sentenced Lula da Silva to jail, along with Marcelo Odebrecht, and continues to prosecute others. Peru has prosecuted two former presidents and others, has jailed Ollanta Humala and his wife, is looking for Alejandro Toledo to be charged for corruption, and has just recently forced PPK to resign from the presidency so that he can be prosecuted.

Partial or High-Level Cover-up. In those countries wherein those implicated control from the executive branch –even if relatively– the legislative and judicial branches, they have conducted partial investigations covering up the main culprits such as; presidents, former presidents, ministers, or other high-level officials, attempting to "sweep under the rug" and charging "escape goats" of lesser rank, as has been denounced and we suspect has happened in the Dominican Republic, Colombia, Panama, Mexico, now Ecuador with Lenin Moreno, and others. In these countries, there is still hope that those implicated will be punished.

Total Cover-up. In countries controlled by Castroist Chavist dictatorships, wherein there is no separation and independence of the branches of government, where there is no Rule of Law, no freedom of the press, and justice is but another tool for the regime, such as; Cuba, Venezuela, Bolivia, Nicaragua, and Rafael Correa's Ecuador, all investigations have been covered-up, they keep them concealed, and there is impunity. Corruption has been denounced with Odebrecht's construction project as the Port of Mariel in the hundreds of millions of dollars, but the Cuban dictatorship covered this up and remains silent. In Bolivia, Evo Morales and his regime cover-up denounced corruption with OAS, Queiroz Galvao, Andrade Gutierrez, and others that even led to the tragic death of the Director of the National Roadway Service, Mr. Jose Maria Bakovic.

To conceal the corruption that has involved the highest levels of government, you need to have lots of power and since those 21st Century Socialism's dictators totally control all power, for now it becomes relatively easy for them to do so. But their nation's people known that corruption is essential for their regimes and are now fighting against it.

A minority President, such as PPK, with a very weak representation in congress, with a strong opposition against him, functioning within a very bureaucratic presidentialist system is doomed to not serve out his term. In my article of 30 May of 2016, under the heading "Peru between Keiko Fujimori and ungovernability" I had predicted PPK's government to be a resounding failure due "to the lack of objective conditions of governance". This situation aggravated by falsehood and corruption, is unsustainable as the facts have shown.

A serious crisis of ungovernability, compounded by corruption, has been waded through without compromising Peru's democracy. The good news is that Peruvian democracy does exist, it works, has shown to be institutionalized, has proven there is Rule of Law, and shows there is separation and independence in the branches of government. There were no rattling of sables; it was a show of civism.

COLOMBIA FOR DEMOCRACY IN LATIN AMERICA

August 10, 2018

Due to its geo-political situation and the regional challenges Colombia is now the center of definition of vital interests for the Americas. Its bordering condition with Venezuela, cocaine production that has surpassed all limits, narco-terrorist guerillas tied to politics, and the threat of the fenced-in but still dangerous Castroist Chavist dictatorial organization that subjects Cuba, Venezuela, Bolivia, Nicaragua are problems for Colombia and for the region. The personal and political conditions of President Ivan Duque create a historic moment that places Colombia in the responsibility of leading the recovery and consolidation of democracy in Latin America.

Among the dangers for the Americas are; narcotics' trafficking, terrorism, organized crime and the people's insecurity, that are precisely the activities that Castroist Chavist regimes from Cuba, Venezuela, Nicaragua, and Bolivia promote, manage, and utilize to keep themselves indefinitely in power.

The narco-state condition of Venezuela with Maduro and Bolivia with Morales, the narco-terrorist activities of the FARC and other groups sustained and defended by the regimes from Cuba, Venezuela, Nicaragua, and Bolivia have been identified. With the Peace Process with the FARC in Colombia the world's cocaine production has grown exponentially to around 200,000 hectares of coca leaf plantations and over 70,000 hectares with Evo Morales and his Coca Leaf Harvester Unions wielding the power of government in Bolivia.

While Evo Morales, on behalf of the dictatorial group, accused at the United Nations in April of 2016 that the war against narcotics' trafficking was "the North American imperialism's instrument of intervention", the increased production of cocaine in Colombia and Bolivia flooded the Americas with drugs, driving the prevalence of consumption in countries such as; Argentina, Brazil, Chile, Mexico, El Salvador, Honduras, Guatemala, and others, enabling the development of drug cartels, "Maras", gangs, and other criminal organizations, thereby increasing the people's insecurity and forcing many to migrate elsewhere.

Venezuela's humanitarian crisis is a problem for the entire region, with special pressure placed on Colombia now turned into a scape route and destination for hundreds of thousands of Venezuelans. Forced migration, encouraged by Maduro's dictatorship, replicates the Castroist technique applied time and again in Cuba with the three-fold objective of; weakening the internal resistance, come up with a cash flow of moneys sent by the exiles, and manipulate the power of negotiation with the offer of stopping the diaspora.

With the leadership of Latin America in the hands of Hugo Chavez and then Fidel and Raul Castro, the 21stCentury in the Americas has been branded by the change of the axis of confrontation of the left with the right to that between dictatorship against democracy. Panama's Summit of the Americas in 2015, marks the time of the dictatorships' greater success over democracy, something that has progressively reverted with milestones such as the OAS' return to its principles with Secretary Almagro, the victory of Macri in Argentina, the impeachment of Rousseff and jailing of Lula for corruption in Brazil, the outcome -still partial outcome- of the "Lava Jato" scandal, the ruining of Venezuela's economy, the change in the United States' foreign policy towards Cuba and other dictatorships, Lima's Summit of the Americas in 2018, the progressive return to democracy in Ecuador with Moreno, and Duque's electoral victory in Colombia.

The recent meeting in Havana of the Forum of Sao Paolo is the last and failed effort of Cuba, Venezuela, Nicaragua, and Bolivia's dictatorships to try keeping their political façade of being "leftist and progressive forces" at a time when the region and the world identify them as bloody "Transnational Organized Crime's regimes" who violate Human Rights on a daily basis.

Latin America faces a time in which the ending of dictatorships is an obligation inherent to international peace and security. The complexity of the battles that remain to be fought range from the imposition of more sanctions, the application of the Palermo Convention, the pursuit of timely diplomatic efforts, credible threats, up to the taking of collective actions. This historic resolution needs a Latin-American leadership backed by the region's and the world's democracies who, due to geopolitical reasons and those of common interest, direct their sight to Colombia's new president.

LATIN AMERICA 17 YEARS AFTER SEPTEMBER 11- 2001

September 12, 2018

Two historic events that have marked the 21st Century happened on 11 September of 2001. The terrorist attack against the United States by the Al-Qaeda network (9/11) and the signing, in Lima, Peru, of the Interamerican Democratic Charter (IDC) by the member states of the Organization of American States (OAS). The terrorist attacks and the reaction to them resulted in dramatic changes throughout the world, and the IDC institutionalized democracy in the Americas. Seventeen years later, the challenge is to revert the negative effects of 9/11 and end dictatorships.

The 9/11 or 11-S (in Spanish) against the U.S. involved four simultaneous suicidal attacks perpetrated by 19 members of the Jihadist network known as Al-Qaeda through the piracy of four commercial aircraft, two of which impacted against the Twin Towers in New York, one crashed into the Pentagon, and a fourth airplane apparently aimed at the U.S. Capitol where they were not successful. That day, they caused 3,016 dead and over 6,000 injured, birthing the global policy of "war against terrorism", the war in Afghanistan and the war in Iraq. They changed the world, from the way passengers board commercial flights, to the development of technology to prevent the reoccurrence of these criminal events.

While in Lima, Peru, the Interamerican Democratic Charter was being signed into adoption as part of a historical event, this was overshadowed by the severity of the terrorist attacks of 9/11.

U.S. Secretary of State, Colin Powell left the Charter signed, before the event, and hurriedly returned to the U.S. The IDC is the result of the most stable period of democracy in the region and when it was signed there was only one dictatorship in the Americas, the Castroist of Cuba. The IDC establishes that "the peoples of the Americas have the right to democracy and their governments have the obligation to promote and defend it" and sets out "the essential components of democracy" among other standards instituted as obligatory.

The intense focus of the U.S. in the war against terrorism and the wars in Afghanistan and Iraq brought about its gradual strategic retreat from Latin America and the absence of a consistent foreign policy for the region. With the rise of Hugo Chavez to power in Venezuela and his immediate alliance with Fidel Castro, there had been since January of 1999, an ongoing process of stabilization and salvage of Cuba's dictatorship and the re-creation -surreptitiously at the beginning- of the failed expansion of the Cuban revolution in the Americas as a "Bolivarian project". These political facts were ignored, dodged, or minimized.

While the U.S. was retreating in its cooperation programs, support to democracy, judicial strengthening, fight against corruption and even antinarcotics and its already fragile means of coordination in military matters, intelligence, and fight against crime, were diminishing, in Latin America vast amounts of money and resources were doled out by Hugo Chavez who, through coup d'états, corruption, populism and a disguise of democracy, was expanding his "ALBA" or Bolivarian project of 21st Century Socialism" known today as "Castroist Chavist".

Far too many of the U.S. and world's "Latin American experts" from the public sector and academia, believed and supported the "democratic and social justice growth" discourse in the Chavez-Castro alliance, when what was truly happening -as the results show today- was the building of; dictatorial regimes who violate freedom and human rights, narco-states justified in the antiimperialist fight, and "Organized Crime's regimes" that control Cuba, Venezuela, Nicaragua, and Bolivia. In Argentina and Brazil, they left the government but not the power, and are a threat to democracies.

A glimpse at the 21st Century thus far in the region shows, as objective reality, a severe regression in democracy, Human Rights and freedom as the result of the successful expansion of "dictatorships of 21st Century Socialism" or Castroist Chavist, who have produced political prisoners and exiles, manipulate justice, commit torture, assassinations, massacres, forced migration, narco-states, economic crises, and a humanitarian crisis. Four Castroist Cubas instead of just one. If we take 11 September of 2001 as a benchmark, we will see that 17 years later, the problems are more severe, the threats more concrete, and the confrontation real.

Hope rests in the fight of the Cuban, Venezuelan, Nicaraguan, and Bolivian people to rescue their freedom and democracy, in decided efforts of democratic governments for their own security, and in the application of the new Foreign Policy of the U.S., that signals a return to the defense of its principles and values that, moreover, coincide with its interests in the region.

ONE OTHER DEMOCRACY AT RISK-PERU IS UNDER CASTROIST CHAVIST ATTACK

October 16, 2018

While the struggle to recoup democracy is focused on the atrocities of the dictatorships from Cuba, Venezuela, Nicaragua, and Bolivia, these regimes carry out a regional plan to sustain themselves. Their dictatorial strategy seeks the greatest destabilization of Americas' democratic governments through social, political, electoral, and criminal meddling and publicity. It is about destabilizing democracy wherever possible and facts now point out that Peru is now enduring the pressures of the application of that agenda.

Hugo Chavez allied himself with Fidel Castro in 1999 when Cuba agonized in its "Special Period" as a parasite state that, since the breakdown of the Soviet Union, did not have a way to survive. With Venezuela's oil, Chavez salvaged the only dictatorship there was at that time in the Americas and kick started the recreation of Castroist expansionism under the labels of Bolivarian Movement, ALBA Project, 21st Century Socialism, and today known as "Castro Chavism".

The 21st Century in Latin America is marked by the influence, expansion, and fall of Castro Chavism identified as an Organized Crime's system that usurps politics. With the Workers' Party with Lula and Rouseff in Brazil, the Kirchner's in Argentina, the ten years of the OAS' subjugation with Insulza, the control of Central America and the Caribbean with Petrocaribe and the FARC from Colombia, they established –amongst other things- history's greatest transnational corruption system. Ranging from the establishment of narco-states and money laundering, to contracts for the construction of mega projects financed by Brazil, with Brazilian companies manipulated by Castro, Chavez, and Lula that brought to light the "Lava Jato" scandal and the "Odebrecht" case.

After having been a victim of Castroist related guerrilla and terrorism, Peru was always a Castro Chavism objective, but they were not able to set up a regime similar to Ecuador's with Correa, Bolivia's with Morales, Venezuela's with Chavez and Maduro, and Nicaragua's with Ortega, where with a populist discourse, supplanting their institutional system, with constitutional reforms and/or constituent assemblies, referendums, annihilated the Rule of Law and concentrated the government's power in order to be able to indefinitely retain it.

With some of Peru's governments, Castro Chavism was able to obtain their vote at international organizations and their support, complicity or indifference to the Human Rights' violations and the breakdown of democracy that Castro and Chavez accomplished in the region. They influenced in the internal politics and electoral processes with relative results. Castroist Chavist's presence in Peruvian politics has not been and is not no less because of the nature of the country and the amount of resources that it has in its antidemocratic quest.

What Castro Chavism was able to accomplish in Peru was to involve it in the corruption scheme of Odebrecht and Lava Jato that led to the fall of President Pablo Kuczynski. The Cuban dictatorship that leads Castro Chavism's efforts, since the death of Chavez, manages machiavelically the corruption scheme because it uses it to cover up its loyal subjects in Cuba, Venezuela, Bolivia, and Nicaragua where the Odebrecht case and Lava Jato and other scams are covered up, but it also applies it as a political weapon in the region such as in the case of the President of Peru PPK.

Lately, Lima's Cardinal and Archbishop Juan Luis Cipriani denounced that "a dark and very strong power is slowly taking over and coincidental events are happening, some stay comfortably in their homes, others stay in jail". Peru's top religious authority points out that "there is a strategy to shut down Congress" and that "the attacks are part of a strategy that was able to destroy the Judicial Branch" claiming that "there is a battle between the three Branches of Government" and pleads for the defense of democracy with the argument that "it is worthwhile to ask for, on behalf of the Rule of Law and on behalf of the country's welfare and the people, some dialogue and no threats either from one side or the other.

The destruction of democracy in Venezuela, Ecuador, Bolivia, Nicaragua and the attempts to do the same in Argentina and Brazil and other countries were abiding by the agenda that now involves Peru. It attacks the multiple political party system, it eliminates civic leaders they Satanize as traditional, they force a collapse of public trust in governmental institutions, they dynamite democracy's prestige and afterwards through populist manipulation they change the country's constitution and eliminate the Rule of Law.

BOLSONARO, VITAL CONTRIBUTION TO DEMOCRACY IN BRAZIL AND IN THE AMERICAS

October 25, 2018

Brazil's democracy has proven to be one of the strongest. Its justice system investigated and prosecuted a worldwide reaching corruption scandal dubbed as "lava jato" with results such as the jail term being served by the former president Lula da Silva. Its Legislative Branch, through a constitutional impeachment, ousted Dilma Rousseff from the presidency. There is freedom of the press and a reliable electoral system. In a crisis, but institutionally vigorous, Brazil points that its next President will be Jair Bolsonaro and offers a vital contribution to democracy in Brazil and elsewhere in the Americas.

Electoral results corroborate the criminal activities of the Workers' Party (PT in Portuguese) as responsible for Brazil's crisis. The governments of the PT used Brazil's monies as credits to other governments so that Brazilian construction companies could engage in the building of mega projects abroad with billions of dollars in surcharges, bribes, and other crimes aimed at expanding and sustaining the dictatorial group of the 21st Century Socialism, or Castroist Chavist system, as an expression of power stemming out of the "Sao Paolo Forum".

For the establishment of 21st Century dictatorships in the Americas, the monies were put up by Venezuela's oil embezzled by Hugo Chavez. With the advent of the PT to the government in Brazil, they added corruption through the mega constructions scheme unveiled with "Lava Jato" and its most important common denominator was "Odebrecht". The third source of funds is narcotics' trafficking with the FARC from Colombia, the Coca Growers Unions of Evo Morales in Bolivia and transnational networks involved in terrorism that identify the dictatorships from Venezuela, Cuba, Bolivia, and Nicaragua as narco-states.

To the resources obtained from Venezuelan oil, PT's corruption, and narcotics' trafficking, as the three main sources of Castroist Chavist funding, we have to add as a direct contribution to Cuba's dictatorship the "contracts for Slave Physicians" and other professionals that include "security", implemented in Brazil by the PT, in Venezuela with Maduro, in Bolivia with Morales, in Ecuador with Correa, in Nicaragua with Ortega, and other countries.

These are some of the reasons why the dictatorships' propaganda portrays Bolsonaro as the "devil on the wall". The advent of Jair Bolsonaro to the Presidency of Brazil is lethal for the dictatorships from Cuba, Venezuela, Bolivia, and Nicaragua, because it speeds up their demise and propels the restoration of democracy throughout the region.

Internally, Bolsonaro will continue towards the complete unveiling of "Lava Jato" and the criminal organization of the PT and the "Forum of Sao Paolo", with greater results in the cleansing and renewing of Brazilian leadership. His administration's agenda is the protection of Brazil's territory and its people from the onslaught of cocaine trafficking from Bolivia and Venezuela, in order to eliminate the lethal damage its causes to the Brazilian people and economy.

Up to now, Brazil's foreign policy regarding PT/Odebrecht activities in the region has been to hand over information Government to Government and this way the regimes from; Cuba, Venezuela, Bolivia, Nicaragua, and Ecuador with Correa, have remained unpunished because these governments are the very ones implicated and they are the ones who have received and control the information. This farce is about to end and the Castro, Maduro, Correa, Morales, and Ortega, along with the Organized Crime sheltered and protected by these governments who falsely brandish the principles of sovereignty and self-determination in order to cover up their crimes, will finally be exposed.

The nearly 13,500 Cuban slaves who serve in Brazil under the program "mais medicos" (more Physicians) that Congressman Bolsonaro was always against, receive about a fourth of the payment that Brazil makes and the Cuban dictatorship takes ownership of the rest. Bolsonaro's plan for this matter is to legalize the stay of Cuban physicians in Brazil, allow for the immigration of their families retained as hostages in Cuba, thus cutting off the millionaire income the Castroist system receives for this crime, with a direct impact on Cuba's GDP (PIB in Spanish).

Bolsonaro's contribution -that the PT's candidate cannot make- to democracy in Brazil and elsewhere in the Americas is to make public the totality of information regarding the "Transnational Organized Crime system" of the PT-Castro-Chavez-Odebrecht scheme covered up until now, that implicates Castro, Chavez, Maduro, Correa, Morales, Ortega and their accomplices; implement the effective protection of Brazil against narcotics' trafficking; and put an end to the exploitation of Cuban slave physicians.

7

ARMED FORCES

IS IT THE OBLIGATION OF THE ARMED FORCES TO REINSTATE DEMOCRACY

January 3, 2018

The year 2017 leaves no doubt there are dictatorships in Cuba, Venezuela, Nicaragua, and Bolivia. They are de-facto regimes that sustain themselves in power through the use of force, violent and judicialized repression, promulgation of "despicable laws" that have supplanted the Rule of Law. Opposition is unfeasible and inexistent because it is exiled, imprisoned, extorted, infiltrated and/or manipulated, without any option to get to power through elections and there is no freedom of the press. Civil resistance and disobedience are brutally repressed. Under these conditions: Is it the obligation of the Armed Forces to reinstate democracy?

Cuba, Venezuela, Nicaragua, and Bolivia are regimes in which human rights are violated with "despicable laws" establishing their retroactive enforcement and penalizing the practice of free professions. This is the mechanism to instill fear in the people with persecutions, hundreds of political prisoners, and thousands of political exiles. The Rule of Law has disappeared by the de-facto institutionalization of an indefinite tenure in and the total control of, all branches of the government. Elections have been depreciated to be only fraudulent rituals controlled by the regime, the universal and secret ballot as an expression of the people's sovereignty has disappeared.

The dictatorship in Cuba goes to extremes to present itself under the ridiculous fallacy of being a "democracy of a single party". In

Venezuela, Nicaragua, and Bolivia there is a nominal opposition for the convenience of the regime, but it is an opposition that is under threat, infiltrated, manipulated and/or simulated, that has no chance whatsoever to get to power through elections. The dictatorship uses such "opposition" to label itself a democracy, even when all components of democracy have disappeared.

The features of these 21st Century Socialism, or Castroist-Chavist dictatorships, are; inefficiency corruption, involvement in narcotics trafficking, declared anti-imperialism (by which they justify their alliance and links with terrorism), exerting control of the government as groups of "organized crime", and their need to remain indefinitely in power in order to have impunity.

Their crimes include; massacres and assassination of members from the opposition and ordinary citizens, judicial manipulation with hatched evidence and false accusations, counterfeiting of legal rules and constitutional supplanting, bribery and kickbacks in the government and state-owned enterprises, submissiveness and treason of the homeland, narcotics trafficking with drug production in the coca-growing zones controlled by Evo Morales in Bolivia and the FARC in Colombia (justified before the United Nations (UN) as anti-imperialistic actions). They are also guilty of; the rigging of economic data which should instead be bona fide, subjecting their people to hunger and misery, increase of crime with their participation or coverup, crimes against humanity, crimes of sexual abuse, trafficking of people, slavery, and more.

In this scenario; Cuba has attacked -or it has allowed attacks- in its territory against foreign diplomats, there are four "Almagro reports" on Venezuela detailing the dictatorial nature of Nicolas Maduro's government, the despicable judges of Evo Morales have acknowledged as a "human right" of the dictator to indefinitely reelect himself, the Ortega's have eliminated the opposition and control the power in perpetuity. In Cuba, Venezuela, Nicaragua, and Bolivia corruption involving Odebrecht and other Brazilian companies that comprised the generation of funds for Sao Paolo forum with Lula and Rousseff that extended bribery throughout the region, is not investigated. All of these countries seek close relations with Islamic regimes, with other dictatorships, and defend North Korea.

The nations of Cuba, Venezuela, Nicaragua, and Bolivia have fallen into a "state of defenselessness". The Armed Forces that should be "the nation's Armed Forces" in other words, of the people, subject to the Constitution, have been turned into "the regime's Armed Forces" and have become the regime's armed sustainment plagued by the submissiveness and corruption of their hierarchy. They have, operating, the "ALBA's Anti-imperialist Military School" in Santa Cruz, Bolivia and have changed all military colleges and institutes' career development curricula and have replaced national military doctrine with the regime's political doctrine. The objective is for the Armed Forces from Venezuela, Nicaragua, and Bolivia to be, at the shortest time possible, similar to those of Cuba, simply stated to become the regime's armed groups.

In a democracy the Armed Forces' loyalty and subordination is owed to the Constitution, but if the government supplants the constitution and oppresses the people, the Armed Forces' loyalty and subordination *cannot* remain deferential to the regime. What is the role of the Armed Forces in current situations such as today's in Cuba, Venezuela, Nicaragua, and Bolivia? Is it the obligation of the Armed Forces to defend the people -of which they are part of-, or the dictatorship? Do the Armed Forces have the obligation to reinstate democracy?

These are the questions asked by citizens and the subjected peoples of Cuba, Venezuela, Nicaragua, and Bolivia. It is a social, political, academic, and international topic on which there is a need for discussion without any biases that may give the advantage to the dictators. It is not about promoting coups d'état, it is about quashing, overturning the overthrows dictators have already perpetrated. It is not about establishing military governments, it is about restoring civilian governments with democracy, and alternation in power. It is not about violating human rights but it is about putting an end to the violation of such rights that are committed daily by the dictators. It is also about restoring the fundamental rights and guarantees of the peoples who are oppressed by force.

CASTROIST CHAVIST DICTATORSHIPS WILL ONLY LEAVE THE GOVERNMENT BY FORCE

July 24, 2018

The regimes from Cuba, Venezuela, Nicaragua, and Bolivia are structured to remain indefinitely in the government, against the will of their people and ignoring international condemnation. Defeated by their people's will, cornered by widespread protests, with crises they have created, buried in corruption and narcotics' trafficking, their daily running of government is a daily chain of crimes they commit and cover up using their political power. Castroist Chavist dictators send, since long time ago, the unmistakable message that they will only leave the government they same way they run it, by force.

No political or democratic act, whether internal or international, has accomplished any change in any of the Castroist Chavist regimes' decision to hold on to the government in perpetuity. In Cuba, the Castro's and their inner circle are the head of a transnational system set up since Hugo Chavez gave away Venezuela's oil and wealth they have used to empower themselves, setting up the dictatorships of Nicolas Maduro in Venezuela, Daniel Ortega/Murillo in Nicaragua, and Evo Morales in Bolivia. In Ecuador they have lost their influence and are suffering their return to democracy.

Cuba's dictatorship is the most remarkable and tragic case with its almost sixty years of shamefulness that is now seeking to strengthen itself with a "constitutional reform" farce, without the people's participation. Among other fallacious ideas they sustain by force, the holders of power in Cuba are deeming convenient to their objective of indefinitely holding on to power, to acknowledge some sort of private property and remove the word "communism" from its text.

Venezuela's dictatorship takes it, as a done deal, its schemed "Constituent Assembly" and "reelection of the dictator" conducted without the people's participation. It endures a growing massive citizens' pressure, Maduro holds on to de-facto power, in spite of his destitution ordered by the National Assembly. The number of political prisoners increases with the arrest of military men and the dictator now plays the old Cuban show of the sixties "to prepare the people for an imperialist invasion". The regime's paramilitary groups spread terror and conduct extrajudicial executions.

Nicaragua's dictatorship, just in these past three months, has assassinated over 350 people, injured over 1,200, imprisoned and exiled political opponents by the hundreds. In order to hold on to power it uses the worn-out resource of "dialogue" that it manipulates to its convenience while conducting "purge operations" with hooded paramilitary thugs that torture, kill, and spread terror against defenders of freedom and all of this while Ortega/Murillo declare themselves to be victims of a "coup d'état" when the entire country is asking them to leave.

Bolivia's dictatorship was just recognized to have turned the country into "the biggest informal economy of the world". It is facing growing massive protests for it to abide by the 21 February of 2016 (21F) referendum through which Evo Morales lost his presumptuousness to be indefinitely reelected, and whose outcome he continues to disavow through a ruling from his judges who have ruled as the dictator's "human right" to be a candidate and commit fraud in perpetuity. In Bolivia, groups of hooded thugs have now appeared claiming to be defenders of Evo Morales and his "process of change" threatening the people who defend the "21F NO means NO" protests. Dictator Morales has asked to "kick to hell" and remove defenders of the 21F and has ordered his paramilitary and coca growers to be on standby alert.

Ecuador's exit from the dictatorial group is attributed to Correa's "mistake" not to be indefinitely reelected and to have instead placed Lenin Moreno as his "controlled candidate" but who, after his election, turned out to be leading his country's return to democracy currently underway. President Moreno called for a referendum and a popular consult that did away with indefinite reelections and is now doing away with "the judicialized political repression" system. He has accused Nicaragua's dictatorship for its criminal acts, has recalled his Ambassador in Bolivia for consultation, and has indicated he will not send an Ambassador to Venezuela.

The acts and strategy of the dictators from Cuba, Venezuela, Nicaragua, and Bolivia to remain forever in power are all the same, the facts reveal this to be a "plan of force" in which crime is the basic instrument and terror and violence are its tools. Castro, Maduro, Ortega/Murillo, and Morales have power by force and are telling the world that the only way they will leave it, is by force.

VENEZUELAN, NICARAGUAN, AND BOLIVIAN ARMED FORCES DEFINE THEIR EXISTENCE

August 23, 2018

At a crucial time for the recovery of democracy and the end of Venezuelan, Nicaraguan, and Bolivian dictatorships, the question is "if the Armed Forces owe obedience to the Constitution or the regime". In democracy the answer is very easy due to the existence of the "Rule of Law", but dictatorships build their military apparatus so that the Armed Forces are solely accountable to the dictator, as in the Cuban model. This is why the Venezuelan, Nicaraguan, and Bolivian Armed Forces define their existence, since they are not part of the process of liberation against dictatorships, the people know they will not be needed.

What for, to have an institution whose objective is the defense of the homeland, of national integrity, of security and service for the people whom they are part of, if when they have to fulfill their role, they do not or worse yet, they support, serve and become a part of the people's oppressor, the criminal system that subjugates the sovereign people?

Cuba's Castroist dictatorship's expansion in the Americas, with the rescue done by Hugo Chavez -embezzling Venezuela's wealth and creating 21st Century Socialism or the Castroist Chavist doctrine- has setup and controls the narco-dictatorial regimes of Nicolas Maduro in Venezuela, Daniel Ortega in Nicaragua, and Evo Morales in Bolivia. The sustainment of these de-facto regimes needs the use of force, reason why it is indispensable to control the Armed Forces, something they have accomplished -up to now- through a misunderstood subordination, corruption, and terror, besides the conformation of irregular and paramilitary armed groups.

It is clearly evident that Venezuela has corrupt military echelons that are part of the regime. The actions and decisions of Padrino Lopez and his surroundings are of a criminal group and not military. They have turned the nation's defense into a mafia that has been so identified by sanctions from the United States, the European Union, the Group of Lima, the OAS, and are in the cross-hairs of counter-narcotics institutions and the Palermo Convention against Organized Crime. They are not out of reach of The Hague either, for crimes against humanity that include the assassination of colleagues who were tortured and fired upon for abiding by their oath and obligation to defend the nation, the homeland. Hundreds of military imprisoned and tortured, accused of conspiring against the regime, are proof the military and the dictatorship's criminal nature.

Nicaragua is a show of cowardice on parade of who, as military, should be an example of courage. Shameful to see the Chief of Staff of the Nicaraguan Armed Forces "declaring himself as neutral" and not defending the people who endure massacres, torture, and crime that Daniel Ortega and his Vice-President and wife Rosario Murillo commit daily. Cowardice, hypocrisy and alibis, because the people accuse the Nicaraguan military for placing soldiers as masked armed paramilitary to massacre. The Nicaraguan military command echelons are committing falsehood, dereliction of duty, and are helping the dictatorship to remain in power. Either they react, or fade into irrelevancy, because important voices such as the former Minister of Defense, Pedro Joaquin Chamorro's have already suggested a post Castroist Chavist Nicaragua without the Armed Forces, and Costa Rica is a good example.

Bolivia, in over 12 years of Evo Morales' dictatorship, has created servile and corrupt command echelons. The dictatorship has taken the task of violating the merit system for promotions in rank, for naming Commanders who are not qualified and who otherwise would never have deserved to be assigned to those positions in a democracy. Corruption is the norm, with rewards for the servile Commanders for their illicit enrichment with positions in Customs Enforcement, embassies, and state-owned enterprises. Cocaine's trafficking to Venezuela in aircraft and with Bolivian military personnel has been exposed by journalist Leonardo Coutinho. The military's servility has even composed a military march to honor the coca grower dictator, placing obsequious lyrics onto a German classical rhythm. The time is coming for the Bolivian military to take a stance and distance itself from the Venezuelans and Nicaraguans. Bolivian people are hopeful that they will live up to be "the Nation's Armed Forces" and not the dictatorship's.

This is only an observation of the objective reality, the social topography. Change is irreversible. Whether this comes about with or without the Armed Forces simply depends on what the military will do, making a choice between crime and the institutional destruction or the fulfillment of their sworn duty.

.

Made in the USA
Monee, IL
10 October 2020